WALKING IN THE SPIRIT

THERE'S POWER IN THE WIND

EVELYN LANG

ISBN 978-1-64114-508-4 (paperback)
ISBN 978-1-64114-509-1 (digital)

Christian Faith Publishing, Inc.
832 Park Avenue
Meadville, PA 16335
www.christianfaithpublishing.com

All scripture is taken from the King James Version of the Bible

Printed in the United States of America

ACKNOWLEDGEMENTS

I would like to thank all the editors at Christian Faith Publishing for their time and patience and doing such a wonderful job. Thanks to my Literary Agent, Brad Lockwood, for all his help in answering my questions and his help in getting this book started.

I would especially like to thank Cassandra Byham for her support as my Publication Specialist, who answered dozens of questions with patience and understanding. Your help was such a blessing to me.

Many thanks to all the staff at Christian Faith Publishing; the copy editors, cover designers, and those in marketing, who have worked so hard on bringing this book to completion.

You are all very appreciated!

To God, who is the Giver of every good and perfect gift.
To Him be the glory for giving me the
privilege of writing this book.

To my husband, Bill, who has many gifts and
talents but whose computer knowledge
I especially appreciated. Thank you. I love you.

To my son Bill, who is always there for me, whose
wise counsel and wisdom I truly appreciate.

To my daughter Melissa, my great encourager, whose
thoughtfulness "spoils" me with my favorite things.

To my daughter-in-law Kristin, whose trust
in God is an example to many.

To my son-in-law, Richard, whose kindness,
generosity and help mean so much to me.

To my grandchildren Rebecca, Allison, Julia, Katharine,
and Mark William – you all are a constant wonder
and blessing to me, precious gifts from God.

God has blessed me with each one of you. I love you.

"Evelyn Lang is like a gentle breeze blowing on one's soul. She is so in tune with the Spirit of God that you want to hear or read about her last conversation with the Lord.

Evelyn's life experiences have qualified her to share her spiritual insight. Others can create that gentle breeze blowing on their life as they read 'Walking in the Spirit – There's Power in the Wind'.

Herman Bailey
Host, Executive Producer of "It's Time for Herman and Sharron"

Walking in the Spirit empowered and inspired me to pursue a deeper level of trust and faith in Jesus Christ. It is a practical guide for all who desire to hear and obey their calling.

Anthony Wood
Founder and CEO Carmen Ministries

"Evelyn Lang has the ability to bring a wonderful human touch to the miraculous working of God in the life of Spirit-filled believers. I trust that her new book "Walking in the Spirit-There's Power in the Wind" will prove a blessing to all those who read it."

Pat Robertson
Founder/Chairman – The Christian Broadcasting Network, Inc.

An excellent book in helping us learn to follow and trust God in practical ways.

Peter Milosky
Assistant Pastor, Beth Israel Worship Center

Profound in its simplicity, and simple yet profound best describes this work of the Lord through Evelyn Lang. Walking in the Spirit is an easy read written in the everyday conversational-like language. Speaking from her spiritual encounters and supported by scripture, the author covers the discerning, managing and nurturing of Spiritual Gifts. This book can be an excellent resource to the Church in the areas of understanding and exercising basic disciplines of the faith i.e. Prayer; study of the Word; rhythms of the spiritual journey (mountain top moments, valley lows and desert experiences); the Deeper-Life and Spiritual Gifts. What a benefit this teaching would be to new and never discipled believers.

Reverend Donna Baptiste
President and CEO Donna Baptiste Ministries;
Host – Pursuing God Radio Program
Associate Pastor (Brooklyn, NY)

CONTENTS

INTRODUCTION

God has given everyone gifts. Even before I became a Born-Again Christian, I knew that God gave people certain natural talents and abilities. However, after I started going to a Holy Spirit–filled church, I also became aware of spiritual gifts. I wanted these gifts too and started asking God to let me hear His voice and also for Him to use me as His vessel. It has been quite an adventure—and not always easy—as I learned that growth has to go right alongside with gifts. You can't have one without the other.

As I look back over the years to the first time I stepped out in faith with a word of healing, I am amused at how little I knew and amazed at how patient God was with me. I didn't want to do anything of my flesh and was very insecure about speaking out. What if I made a mistake? Would God be mad at me? How could I be sure it was Him Who was speaking to me?

When I first started hearing God, I asked Him who or what situation He wanted to heal. The words came, and then just as quickly came the doubts. I kept asking, even as time went on, "Is this You Lord?" Finally, after many weeks and maybe even months of asking this every time I got a word, all of a sudden, I heard the words of response to me in my mind, "*Well, who did you ask?*"

I had to chuckle as those words made everything so simple. God has a sense of humor! Sometimes we complicate things, and sometimes we let the enemy put fear in us. Either way, it prevents us from speaking what God tells us. Of course, we don't want to do anything of our flesh—or speak lightly or irresponsibly. We want to be responsible. However, we also can't be paralyzed with fear of making a mistake.

We do our responsible best and speak with humility, telling the receiver to test the word. God will usually use us to confirm something the person already knows. If it's a healing word, we will see fruit. Jeremiah 32:6–8 shows us that even the prophet Jeremiah wasn't sure at all times, that it was God speaking to him. Learning isn't always easy—in fact, it usually never is. We all have some growing pains.

I pray that this book will help answer questions that you may have as well as encourage you to step out into all that God has for you as His vessel.

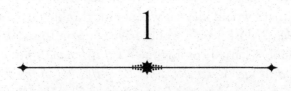

1

OBEDIENCE

RAINFALL STARTS WITH ONE DROP

Everything starts with obedience. When God gave me my first word of healing, I had a choice—do I step out and speak it or do I let fear come in? It seems to be an easy decision, but I wrestled with it all through our worship service at church. As I look back on it now, I have to laugh at my insecurity, but I am also amazed at the patience God had with me. I tell this story to you now because many of you may be able to relate to it, even though it is somewhat embarrassing to me to have questioned God as I did.

I had asked God for a word of healing that Sunday morning. I had been getting words of prophecy for some time but never a word of healing. God had put in my heart a desire for people to be healed. When I asked God for a word, immediately I heard, "If I give you a word, will you speak it, even if you don't know of anyone who has it?"

The church I attended was very small, and everyone knew each other well. I responded that, yes, as long as I knew it was God and not my flesh, I would speak it. The word *eye* came to mind right away. I then reasoned that I could have thought of that myself, so I asked God if I could have something more specific about the eye.

Instantly, *fluid build-up* came to mind. Well, that was pretty specific, so I went on to ask if there was anything else God wanted to heal. Again, the word came—*knee*. And again, I reasoned, *Well, I could have thought of that myself*, so I asked if there was something specific so that I would know it was not me thinking it. Immediately, I got *cartilage*. Most people would have gone on to speak it but not me. The doubts started coming in. *What if I made a mistake? Would God be mad at me? What if I were doing this out of my flesh because the words did come in my mind?* So, I said to God that if it were Him speaking to me, to please confirm it by having our pastor say something about healing. (What chutzpa!)

Within minutes, a man on the worship team began talking about how God wants to heal. Did I take this as confirmation? Not me. I said, "Lord, I asked that if it were You speaking to me, that the *pastor* would have a word, not someone else, so I'm still not sure if it is You I am hearing. Please have Pastor say it." Again, the man on the worship team talked about healing. So, again, I asked God to have Pastor say it.

This time, our pastor did. How did I respond? I said, "But, Lord, I don't know of anyone here with these problems!" All of a sudden, I heard, "Didn't you tell Me that you would speak it even if you didn't think anyone had it?" My heart must have skipped a beat as I went forward with the word. As I spoke it, a man in the congregation confirmed the word, and someone's knee was healed that very service. Another person came up for fluid build-up in the eyes.

God is so kind to us. He knows us better than we know ourselves, for I didn't realize that I would have had such fear and doubt come in and need such confirmations. However, even though I needed a big push, God helped me to be obedient. And since then, He has been teaching me and helping me grow in the gifts He's given me.

Did I get confidence right away? *No!* There are times when I still struggle when I get a word I don't understand and try to reason it out. But I am doing much better. I have learned to follow my heart, for the Lord lives in it. I try not to let fear, or my reasoning, lead me. I've always seen that when I get a word from my heart, and fear comes in to get me to not speak the word, as I overcome the fear and speak it, it was exactly the word that someone needed. I find that when God desires to do something special in someone's life, the more the enemy will try to get you to doubt you have heard from the Lord or to get you to fear making a mistake. If we follow our heart, that's where the treasure lies. If we follow our mind, no matter how logical it may seem, no treasure will come from it, for it is flesh.

Now, if He can do this for me, He can do this for you. All that is required is obedience. Out of obedience comes God's favor and reward. Sometimes, all it takes is our yes (to God) to have His.

One main reason why people don't use the gifts is that they don't know they have them. Many feel that God could never use them. However, all it takes is a willing heart that will yield to God. It takes a heart that listens. God speaks to all, but not all hear Him. It takes death to self and total surrender to His Spirit. It starts out small—maybe only one word—and if you obey and speak it, more will come. Who will step out of their comfort zone? Who will yield to God's heart? God is no respecter of persons; His gifts are for everyone. It is our choice whether or not to obey.

The gifts are not for the people who deliver the word; they are for others. God speaks to us about our own needs in our prayer time. But the gifts God gives us are really for others' benefit. Do we have God's heart for others? Do we want more for others than for ourselves? God gives words to and for us in our prayer time with Him—the anointing and gifts are given for others. That is the way we are used as God's vessels. That is God's time to reach out to others through us. Are we willing? Will we obey?

What is the reason we desire to be used in the gifts? Is it for recognition? Or is it a desire because of a genuine love and concern for others? The reason behind the motivation is what counts.

The gifts of the Holy Spirit are to help others, but when we allow ourselves to be used in the gifts, we have a closer relationship with the Lord so that He guides us and talks to us in our prayers. Our hearts are like big pottery vessels that can be filled with rain. God wants to fill our spiritual vessels up. The more we desire Him, the more He will fill us. He wants to fill us to overflowing so that we can pour out to others, and then He will fill us back up again. God always wants to fill us up and sends the rain down, but sometimes the rain falls by the wayside and is not caught in the vessel. Sometimes, there is no vessel to catch the rain because our hearts are not turned to Him. All those whose hearts are turned to God receive from Him.

God has given us all gifts—all we have to do is to tap into them. How do we do this? We do this by asking God. Moses asked the Lord for water, and when God told him to tap the rock, water gushed out (Exod. 17:4–6). We tap into the gifts by asking God for them. They were there all the while from before we came into being. All that God has given us has been given before time began; we already have it, and as we seek the Lord, He will make us aware of it. We just have to unlock the door. We do this by seeking and asking. God says to call unto Him and He will tell us great and mighty things (Jer. 33:3). He tells us to ask and we shall receive, seek and we shall find, knock and the door shall be opened to us (Matt. 7:7). These scriptures tell us what we need to do—ask. Then we need to keep asking, seeking, and knocking; and God will continue to give us pearls of wisdom as we unlock the doors to hidden treasures.

When we are new, we ask, "Is this You, Lord?" God will tell us. We see whether it is God by the fruit of it. As we see the fruit, then our confidence in hearing the Lord grows. First, we step out in faith and we obey; and as we see the fruit, it becomes easier and easier for us to recognize the Lord and the gifts He has given us. Everyone is different and grows differently, but God does what is best for each one. He is not a "cookie cutter" God, so He will use us each in different gifts and each according to our own personalities. We should never compare ourselves to one another. He uses each one in the way that demands it.

I can remember a time when I would hear someone praying in the Spirit and wonder, *Why don't I sound like that?* I also wondered if they heard the Lord differently than I did. God asked me why I made it so complicated. Why did I think hearing from Him has to be different than talking to a friend? He asked me why I wanted to be and hear like someone else when He has given me a special gift? He said that He created each one differently, each with a different personality. So, we need to just receive what He gives us the way He gives it to us—that is, according to our own special personality. We should not model ourselves after someone else, for each one of us is special in God's sight. I was then reminded of a friend who once told me that the idea of perfection that I had for myself isn't necessarily God's idea of perfection.

Another time, while I was still so insecure, I heard a man say that he always knows it's the Lord because when the Lord gives him a word, he sounds so unlike himself. He used *thee*s and *thou*s, etc. Well, I always sounded just like myself in the words that came out. They were usually things I had not thought of before, but they were expressed in the way that I usually spoke. This made me very unconfident, and as I asked God about this, again, I got that He does what He wants and that He gives me words the way He wants.

He said that I had many confirmations that the words I had gotten were the words of the Lord and not my flesh. (I used to ask for confirmations all the time and usually someone would respond, so the fruits were there. One time, I even had someone come up to me and say that God told them to tell me that it was Him I was hearing from!) Still, I was very insecure and afraid to make a mistake. At one point, in comparing myself to someone else, I got, "Does the cup complain that it's not a saucer?" It took time, but I finally began to recognize and be confident that it was the Lord I was hearing from, whether I sounded like someone else or not!

God always wants to bring us to a new level and a new dimension of Him. Just as a parent coaxes a child to walk, so God coaxes us to new levels in Him. But each time, it takes a stretching, a step of faith. *We* have to *choose* to step out of our comfort zone. God will not make that decision for us. But as we step out, He is right there, coaxing, encouraging us. What we then see is that although we stepped into a new level, we did not step out on our own but stepped into a greater relationship with Him. He pushes us along in faith to step out as His vessel; and when we do, we come into that closer relationship. It's like a parent pushing a child on a swing. He pushes us out, we come back to Him knowing more of Him, and so on.

So many are afraid to swing high. They want to stay put and don't want to go to higher levels. That's OK. God loves them too. But I wonder if they will have the joy that comes as a child swings high and his spirit soars.

When God finds someone who will obey and speak His word, He will give that person more. If we don't speak it, He will find someone who will. At first, it may just be one word. As God told me one time, rainfall starts with one drop!

We also need to learn to recognize the difference between what the Lord is telling us and our flesh, and then we need to be able to interpret what God is telling us accurately. This is not easy, especially when we are learning. I think it is easier for a baby to learn something than we as adults because a baby doesn't have to unlearn things first! We need to learn how to shut off our minds—our intelligence and logic—to hear God. Sometimes, we are even at the halfway point, sometimes being able to shut down our minds only to find our own thoughts coming back in. It takes more time for some than for others to overcome this. We should not be discouraged, however, when we are not sure if it's our flesh or not, for even Jeremiah wasn't sure it was God at times (Jer. 32:6–8).

Jeremiah had gotten a word from the Lord that his uncle's son will come to him, asking him to buy a field. After he came and asked him, Jeremiah said that then he knew it was the word of the Lord. Recognizing God's voice is about knowing where our thoughts come from. God speaks in many ways. (I go into more detail about this in *Lessons I learned from the Lord.*) There's His audible voice, which does not sound like our own. God will usually use that voice at times of urgency or great importance. Sometimes, He speaks in that still, small voice; and sometimes, He gives us "knowings" about something or someone. Sometimes, He speaks to us in our mind.

It may sound like it could be our thought because He is in us. But we know it is the Lord because He gives us wisdom, knowledge, and revelation we would not otherwise know. He sometimes speaks a word in a flash or gives us a picture. We know it is the Lord in all instances by the fruit of it. We know it is His voice because it is comforting and gentle. The enemy's voice puts in fear, guilt, or condemnation. If God spoke to us like thunder, we would be afraid, like the Israelites were when they told Moses to talk to God and tell them what He said (Exod. 20:19).

The Holy Spirit speaks softly and gently. He teaches and comforts. He gives us wisdom. This is the fruit of His words. One time, when I asked God if it was Him speaking to me, He responded by saying to me, "Well, whom did you ask?" The enemy will put in your mind unasked, unwanted words. When you ask the Lord, He is the one to respond.

When I first began moving in the gifts of the Holy Spirit, I had a knowing in my spirit and I did not know it was also a word from the Lord. I felt God's love for His people so strongly that it was inexpressible. I just *knew* His compassion for us. Since I did not get any words, I told the pastor later about what I felt, and he explained that the Holy Spirit was putting a message in my heart. I felt so bad that I did not say anything, for then I knew that God wanted His people to understand His great love for them. The pastor then told me that God understands that we are just learning, and he incorporated it in his sermon. So, the message got through anyway. Looking back on it all, I see how we grow as we step out and experience all these different ways God talks to us.

One of the biggest hurdles I had to get over was when I would get the same word of healing I got a few days or even a few weeks before. I would wonder if it was my flesh, and then fear would come in to prevent me from speaking it. As I look back, I can see how silly this was, for there is not only one person with that same problem!

As I gained confidence and spoke the word, I would find this out to be true, over and over again. One time in church, a lady came up to me before the service and told me she had an earache. During worship, I felt God was giving me a word about someone's ear. But then, I thought it could be my mind remembering what that lady had told me. I struggled with it for quite some time until I felt like I really needed to say it. When I did, a different person came up for prayer for their ear!

This was one of the first lessons I learned about using my own logic, yet I did not want to do anything of my flesh or make a mistake. I wanted to be very responsible in using what God gave me. The problem was, I was so afraid of doing anything of my flesh, I would try to "reason" it out! Even though I felt God's anointing, and when I first got the word, sensed it was the Lord. When you let your mind take over, you can't hear God. You're choosing your own reasoning over His voice.

Sometimes, God would give me a picture that led to a prophetic word. Again, if I got the same picture a month later, even though I was not thinking about it, I would wrestle with whether or not it was my flesh. But in this too, the same picture could have two different messages.

An example of this is, when one day, God gave me a picture of big red lips. The word with that picture was of being careful of what comes out of our mouths. It must have been several months later when I saw those lips again. I dismissed it without even asking God about it because I reasoned it out to be my mind just remembering the previous word. The next day, I saw those lips again. God was trying to get something through to me that I was obviously resisting.

This time, I asked the Lord what He was trying to tell me. It was a message of love. So, I asked the Lord, How do I tell when I'm remembering something in my mind and when You are telling me something different, when I'm getting the same word or picture? The answer I got was so simple—don't think, just receive! If you do what *you* think, there's no power. If you do what God *says*, you will see His power and signs and wonders. Then I asked God to help me to do this and to teach me not to reason.

Now, when we ask God to do something, He always does. Usually, I have found that He does it when I'm not expecting Him to. I know this is how He has to teach me because He knows, if I think something could be my thought, I'll reject it. So, several weeks later, I was with a friend who had her grandchildren visiting. The little one had a pacifier. The next day in prayer, sure enough, what do I see in my mind's eye, but a pacifier. I thought at first it was just that I was remembering again, but this time, I started getting a teaching with it.

After the teaching, God had me realize that when I saw the pacifier, I immediately thought it was just my flesh remembering the day before. He revealed to me that I had asked Him to teach me how to know the difference of when it was just my own mind remembering and when it was the Lord showing me something. I did not shut out the pacifier thought immediately as I had been doing but asked God about it. He was able to teach me two things as a result. The first was the teaching about God being with us always. The second thing was that we should not reason it out when a thought comes in, just ask and receive.

It is a tendency of human nature to try to reason things out. However, our logic and reasoning is our enemy when it is in regard to speaking a word from God. We need to just say it like we got it, not putting our own thoughts on it. I remember one time when I first started getting healing words from the Lord, I got a picture of an X-ray of bones; and I got the impression that it was of the arm, from the elbow to the wrist.

When the word was spoken, a man said he knew of someone with a broken leg, and I started to question whether or not I heard correctly about the arm. But right after that, two people came forward with bandaged wrists. So, I learned not to question but to take the word I got at face value. It was part of the process of having confidence in what I was hearing was indeed from the Lord and not wavering but trusting that what I was hearing was from the Lord.

A slightly different way I reasoned came about the same time as the X-ray word. As I got to church, a lady came up to me and told me that she had a bad cold. Later during the church service, I got a word about mucous. I naturally thought it must be my flesh because that lady told me she had a cold. But then I started to realize that if it were my mind, I would have gotten the word *cold*. So, I asked God and got the impression that He wanted me to say it. Someone else responded to that word, not the lady with the cold. I was beginning to know that I shouldn't think! The minute we try to reason it out in our own minds, we give the enemy an open door to put in confusion and to complicate the word. Keep it simple.

As God uses us, we will go through struggles—fear of making mistakes, wondering if we heard correctly, being humbled, and maybe even looking foolish at times. There is a price to pay to be used by God. It means going through the struggles and standing strong. It means not giving up. God uses all these things so that we will be able to speak what He tells us with boldness and authority. There is trial and error in learning.

God showed me a river after a heavy rain. The water was all muddy. But then after a while, the bottom settles down again and the water becomes clear. This happens to us sometimes. As God increases the anointing in us, things buried on the bottom are purged up (unforgiveness, bitterness, etc.). We get confused as the enemy attacks. After the junk on the bottom has been purged, the waters become clear, and we have more clarity than before. Clarity comes with familiarity as we become close to Him. It takes time. We should never give up on ourselves. God doesn't give up on us, we shouldn't either.

I will tell you the teaching I got about the pacifier because God is so awesome; He tells us things that are interwoven, even when we don't see it at first. I realized later that in this teaching, He was showing me that all I need to do is depend on Him and not to fear, even when I am afraid of making a mistake and doing something of my flesh. He was asking me if I saw the child with his pacifier. He told me that the pacifier is his security, his comfort, and his peace. He then told me that He is our security, our comfort, and our peace. He told me to depend on Him, like the child needs that pacifier. He showed me that the child did not let go of that pacifier, not even for a minute. He made sure he had it at all times. God wants us to not let go of Him for a minute, to keep Him with us at all times. When fear comes in, we let go of faith.

As we grow, we learn to push fear away and hold on to faith and the Lord. What we don't realize sometimes is that although we may let go of our grip, God never lets go of His grip on us. Just like a child who has a pacifier pinned to his shirt, it may fall out of his mouth, but it still is on him. So, even when we let go of faith and let fear come in, He is still with us. He will never leave us or forsake us. It is not what we *feel*; it is who God *is*.

Because I was so unconfident in the beginning, I kept asking God to give me more discernment and even confirmations. I was very afraid of making a mistake or doing something of my flesh. My heart would pound, and my knees shake as I delivered the word God gave me. I was out of my comfort zone. The enemy was constantly putting in doubts and fear. However, God was seeing if I would speak His word and not get discouraged or give up—even when out of my comfort zone, even when the enemy would put in fear.

When God sees we will stand strong and obey, then He knows He can trust us to give His word regardless of where we are or the circumstances, and then He will give us more. The Lord knows us, and He knows if we truly are concerned whether or not something came of our flesh. He knows if it is intentional or not. He does not mind if we make a mistake of the flesh because we don't know it's our flesh. He does mind if we *know* it's our flesh and say it anyway. That's intentional false prophecy.

If we're not sure, all we have to do is ask the Lord and not try to reason it out in our own mind. We don't have to analyze the word ten different ways before we speak it. Just ask! Those who do things intentionally out of their flesh never even think about it because it doesn't bother them whether or not it's their flesh. It's performance and counterfeit. That is why God chooses responsible people who do their best to make sure it is the Lord they are hearing from. We are all human, and we will make mistakes. But if we press on and do our very best for the Lord, we will be amazed at the ways He will use us.

What about when we get a word from someone and we're not sure if it's from the Lord or their flesh? Ask the Lord! It is a scare tactic of the enemy to make us believe it's wrong to question whether or not a word is from the Lord. We are to test everything (1 Thess. 5:21; 1 John 4:1). Everyone can make a mistake. Many times, we get confused (confusion is also from the enemy) about childlike faith. Childlike faith is believing God's word when He has given us a promise—that He is faithful to perform it—and not questioning or doubting whether He will do it. But when someone else tells us something that they think is from the Lord and it's not a confirmation of what God has told us, we need to have discernment. If we are not sure, we should then ask the Lord if it is of Him or not.

This is very important, for there will be mistakes as well as those that are counterfeit. If the enemy can make us think that it is wrong to question a word, then we can be deceived easily. We will think that something is from the Lord when it is not and vice versa. When we wonder if the person heard correctly, we are not questioning the Lord; we are questioning *where* it's coming from. You're simply asking God if it's from Him or not. If God tells you it's Him, believe it. If He tells you it's not, don't. It's one thing for us to judge the word for ourselves; it's another thing to ask the Lord. Discernment is the Holy Spirit telling you what is from where—in effect, it's the Lord telling you before we ask! If we don't have discernment about something, then ask. Ask with confidence and not fear. It's as simple as that.

What do we do when someone we trust gives us a prophetic word that is not a confirmation of what God has already spoken to us about? We should not immediately reject it without asking God about it first just because it's a new word to us. Or maybe it is something that we think we are not capable of doing. Just because we think that we cannot do it doesn't mean that God can't. Just because we can't imagine something doesn't mean that God doesn't have it for us.

When I received a word that I was going to write my first book, *Lessons I learned from the Lord*, it was something I thought I could never do. I'm so thankful that I did not immediately reject the word as flesh but, instead, asked the Lord if it was indeed His plan for me.

2

✦⋯⋯✺⋯⋯✦

REVELATION

THE GREAT AWAKENING

Ah, slumber is sweet—but the alarm is ringing! We as Christians need to be awakened to our kingdom purposes. We have to be aware of all God has for us before we can receive it. How many of us go through life in a state of slumber, never knowing what God has for us?

The most important revelation area we need growth in is revelation of God's love for us. There are stages in love—growth periods when we get a fresh infilling and a greater revelation of love, a greater level of love, and a new awareness of that love. It's an expansion of love that increases when we are aware of it. For example, there are times in married couples' lives when they're so busy that they have to make sure that love is not crowded out by that busyness. There are also times when a greater love just wells up inside of them for each other, and they have a new infilling of that love that gives them a greater awareness, and love is increased. God wants to bring us to that greater awareness and increase of His love for us.

REVELATION PRECEDES RECEPTION

As children, we had many desires. We all want to be successful in reaching our childhood dreams. What we don't often realize is that if we delight in God, He gives us the desires of our hearts (Ps. 37:4). When He says that He gives us the desires of our heart, I see two meanings. One meaning is that He puts them there; He gives us the desire in the first place. And the second meaning is that He brings them about. However, whatever God puts in your heart needs to be watered. What the desires are watered with determines the result. If they are watered with the world, they will not thrive. Ungodly principles will lead to destruction. When they are watered in the Word, using Godly principles, they will grow to maturity. How long it takes for them to grow depends upon how long it takes for us to learn these principles and how long it takes for us to walk in them after we learn.

Knowing what to do is one thing; doing them is another story. And once we start learning and doing, it is a never-ending flow. Knowledge leads to doing, which leads to more knowledge and so on. For example, a new farmer has some knowledge of planting. However, as the years go by, he learns more about the soil, fertilizing, the plants, and what works best with those plants. Each year, he learns to produce a better crop. There is so much to learn about the peanut! We continue to learn in the spirit also.

As we learn one principle in a scripture and start acting upon it, we are then taken to a new level of understanding of that same scripture. We then grow in greater knowledge and understanding of it. We don't just stop at the surface when we have some knowledge. Just when we think we know everything, God reveals more.

As God was teaching me about this one day, He showed me a beautiful crystal wineglass. He told me that we are His vessels and He fills us up with wine, which I understood to mean wisdom and knowledge. Unlike wine in the natural, we should never say we have enough, for then the growth stops. Just like the woman with the pots, we should keep bringing Him more to fill so that He can expand our knowledge of Him (2 Kings 4:1–6).

Our desire should be to want more of God and never be satisfied with what we have of Him—what our knowledge is of Him. We should want to be like lovers who desire to know everything about each other. Those of us who are in love spend every waking hour thinking about the one we love and can hardly wait to be in their presence. Seek the Lord like that, continually adding more of Him, for He wants to fill us up. As He was telling me this, I had to smile as He said that He warns us; He can be intoxicating!

When I was praying, God revealed His heart to me regarding wisdom. He was saying that He holds the key; and as He teaches us, and we learn and obey, we receive the key. The key opens the door to unlock the treasures He has for us—wisdom, knowledge, and revelation. It is the key to His heart. As we seek Him, we will find Him. As we knock, the door will be opened. So, as we seek Him, we learn about Him. As we learn about Him, we love Him more. As we love Him, we obey Him and do what He has taught us. Then we get more wisdom, more knowledge, and more revelation of His heart. It's our choice as to how much we want. All it takes for us to receive wisdom is to *ask*. Many do not ask.

I wonder why they are comfortable where they are and are afraid to move forward. Why are they satisfied with so little? God desires to give everyone gifts. He is not a respecter of persons. He desires to give wisdom, but He is not asked. We desire material things; and it's not wrong to want nice things, if these things are not most important. Remember what the Word says: "But seek ye first the kingdom of God, and His righteousness; and all these things shall be added unto you" (Matt. 6:33).

God wants to give us His good treasures, but many look to other sources. He wants our desire to be more of Him. Then as we desire Him, He helps us in all we do. How many, in desiring what the world has to offer, have heaps of debt piled upon them by not having wisdom with credit cards? Yet God will give us favor in all learning and knowledge. And when God gives, He gives freely—out of love. All He requires is our love. He says to come to Him, for He holds the keys.

As long as we are willing to learn and grow, we will. As long as we know that we don't know, then we will begin to know. Things are not always what they seem. A know-it-all knows nothing at all, for he goes by his own wisdom and gives himself credit for what he does know. Fool! The wise understand that to know is to know the One, the Creator Who is the source of all wisdom. God gives wisdom to those who seek Him. So, to grow wise is to seek the One Who is Wise, not man who is but dust. Everything we need to know, God gives us, just for the asking. He gives us revelation knowledge.

Many times, this means changing our thinking—letting everything we used to know, our own wisdom that we depended on—fall to the ground and letting God take over. He will tell us things that are different than what we now know. To walk in all He has for us means letting go of all we know and yielding to Him. At times, God tells us *what* He's going to do; but instead of waiting for Him and His timing, we help Him out and try to make it happen in our own way and time. But if we yield our minds to Him, He will tell us *how*. If we yield to Him, He will give us new ideas and new ways of doing things. It's hard to let go of the old familiar ways, but if we do this, God will do a new thing in us.

God gives us revelation by being in His Word and in our prayer times with Him. He is the Great Teacher, and all wisdom comes from Him. He also gives us signs. We see signs in the natural all the time and we follow them. If we see black clouds in the sky, we bring an umbrella with us when we go outside. When we see buds on the trees, we know it's spring. But do we see the signs that God gives us personally for our lives?

He wants to give us direction to get to the place He has for us. He has our future all mapped out for us (Ps. 139). He gives us direct routes, but so often, we are like mice in a maze, wanting to get somewhere but not knowing which path to take. He is the Way, the Truth and the Life (John 14:6). His voice leads us and guides us. It is the beacon in the night, the radar in the day. All we have to do is look, seek and ask, and then listen. He wants to reveal His plans to us and then tell us how to get there. He wants to give us more clarity.

Coming to the Lord as a child is the secret, for we need to stay as a child in order to grow! Things of the spirit are opposite things of the flesh. It seems totally contrary to what we are taught in the natural. As we remain humble as a child, then pride can't come in, for then we won't think anything is of our own doing or knowledge. That is when God can work His best in us. A know-it-all leaves no room for growth. They think they know everything already. God works with those who give Him room to work. Those that don't give God *room* in their lives won't see His *work* in their lives. Pride sneaks in silently and slowly. Those who watch out for it won't be deceived.

We also need to know the difference between pride and feeling special as God's child. Pride boasts and thinks I did it myself. Pride is when we want glory for ourselves. That's different from feeling loved and special because we've heard from the Lord. Pride is unreasonable conceit of superiority—it is self-glorifying. Feeling special is when we know we are regarded with particular favor and affection (*Webster's Third New International Dictionary*).

We have only seen the tip of the iceberg. Most of it is below the water. As we learn, we see more and more below the surface. We understand more about parables and scriptures. We learn things hidden. They are revealed to us as we dig deeper and go deeper in understanding. Mysteries are revealed. And revelation produces understanding, which increases faith to believe. Just when you think you know it all, more is revealed.

That is why we need to hunger and thirst after God (Matt. 5:6). Hunger is not satisfied until it is full. And once full, in a little while, hunger returns. Hunger is needed for growth. As the body needs food to grow, so does the spirit. It needs to be hungry to grow. In times of hunger, we seek God more. It is at those times that we will go deeper in understanding. You can't just eat once and be satisfied. To read scripture and understand in your mind is to just touch the surface, the tip of the iceberg. But as you grow, more and more is revealed and understanding deepens. It is not by human intellect but by the revelation of God. It becomes rhema. That is spiritual growth. And when you know that you don't know it all, that is when the journey begins.

That is why those who think they are wise are foolish, and God uses the foolish to confound the wise (1 Cor. 1:27). Relish the journey, for it is the journey that helps us grow. Once we get there, we start over again on the next one. Enjoy each step of the way, for that is what life is about. When we learn to enjoy the journey, we have peace and enjoy more. Otherwise, life just rushes by, going from one thing to another, not appreciating what's there for the moment.

Savor each moment. When we bite a morsel, we can chew it slowly and savor the taste, or we can swallow it whole, hardly tasting it at all. Relish it—don't let life pass you by. As the Bible says, "O taste and see that the Lord is good: blessed is the man that trusteth in him" (Ps. 34:8).

As we grow in revelation and knowledge, there are different levels of understanding. With revelation, we go deeper; with growth, we go higher. The levels of revelation go down, not up because they go from head to heart. It is a continual process of learning. You may think you know all about a scripture or a spiritual gift, and then all of a sudden, revelation comes and you know it in a deeper way. It is an understanding that increases faith and growth in that area. It is a new dimension of understanding. It is not so much a higher level of growth but a deeper revelation of the wisdom and knowledge God has already given you.

An example of this would be if you were learning to high dive. You start out on a board that is not so high and dive into the water. When you have grown to master this level, you go on to a higher board. With each new level of height, you go deeper in the water as you dive in. The higher up you go in spiritual growth, the deeper you go in revelation. You can't go higher again until you go deeper in wisdom, revelation, and knowledge in that area of growth. When we go to a new level in growth, we can choose to remain on that diving board (level) and look at the surface of the water, or we can choose to jump in and go deeper in understanding. But unless we jump in and get off that diving board, there is no way to get to the higher one. Things are not always what they seem—we must go higher to go deeper and vice versa!

It's not always comfortable to go higher. We have reached a maturity level, and sometimes we want to stay there. And sometimes we want more for someone else than they want for themselves. It is the same with God—He always wants more for us than we want for ourselves. But unless the person wants as much as we want for them, it won't happen, no matter how much *we* try.

If we are disappointed that the person isn't interested in being all that he can be, how much more must God be disappointed when we don't want to become all He wants us to be? When we don't have the desire to grow, we won't. God even wants to give us the desire, but we don't always want to accept it. How frustrating it must be! Just as it doesn't work when we want more for someone than they do, it doesn't work when God wants more for us than we do. It is all up to us. Are we willing to do what it takes on our part? Are we willing to make the effort?

We want things handed to us on a silver platter. But anything gotten that easily doesn't require any growth on our part and is therefore lost easily. Easy come, easy go. I have heard of so many lottery millionaires that because they are unprepared to deal with wealth, many times, become worse off than they were before. God prepares us by a growth process to be able to handle all He gives us. This takes time and sometimes trials, but in the end, we become mature enough to handle it and not get into trouble.

God gives us revelation in words of knowledge and wisdom, and He also gives us revelation in His written Word. God's Word gives victory and life. It is powerful. When we understand the power of God's Word, we can declare the victory over any situation. For example, if we have a sickness, we may receive a word of knowledge for our healing, or we may read a scripture that becomes rhema to us. There's power in God's Word. It is protection, health, blessings, provision—it is *wholeness*. It is comfort and peace to our emotions. It is everything we need. As soon as we understand the power of God's Word, then we can declare it and receive what it says for us personally. As the Word says, "There shall no evil befall thee, neither shall any plague come nigh thy dwelling" (Ps. 91:10).

An important thing to remember when declaring scripture is to let faith be behind our words and not fear. Faith is the fuel behind the Word. When you declare scripture with faith, you are saying my God is Able, and you see results. When we declare scripture with fear behind it, the fear causes doubt to water down the Word and put out the fire (power) behind it. How do we replace fear with faith? Just say God is Able or just say a scripture that builds your faith until the fear goes. Matthew 17:20 states that if we have faith as a grain of mustard seed, we can speak to the mountain and command it to go and that nothing shall be impossible to us. Let faith, not fear, be the motivation because fear can cloud our minds, even when we are declaring God's Word.

God's Word has substance. That means His Words are real, true, not imaginary. They are solid, firm, and existing. God's Word and promises are real! They exist as substance. When we take hold of this, our faith becomes strong.

People will use God's Word without understanding its power; therefore, they speak it without confidence. They speak it without boldness and authority because they don't really believe what it can do. They hope; they don't *know*. The enemy knows whether or not we understand the power or not. He knows when you only half believe. He knows when you speak it with confidence. He's a bully and, like all bullies, will run when confronted with a bigger force than he. When we realize that Jesus died on the cross, not only to free us from the bondage of sin but also to give us back the dominion that Adam lost when he sinned, we can walk in the authority that Jesus gave to us. It is ours for the taking. We take it by revelation. It is revelation that leads to perception that destroys deception. If Satan can deceive us and cloud our perception, he can hold dominion over us. But once we have the revelation that Jesus gave dominion back to us, we can walk in all He has for us.

As we grow spiritually, the power of God's Word sinks in, and we start speaking with more authority each time we use it and see results. Our faith becomes stronger. We have to understand the power in order to use it properly. When electricians work with heavy voltage lines, they have to understand how the power works so that it can be used effectively. When we realize that God is the Word and that we are His children and He has given us His authority, then we can speak His Word with confidence and know that His Word produces results. The enemy is frightened of people who know who they are in Christ. We just have to always remember to never let pride come in. It is because of to Whom we belong and nothing we have done.

When I asked God how I could understand this in my heart more and to have more faith in the power of His Word for me, He told me that He is the Word and we are His inheritance; therefore,

His promises are for us. We only need to understand the power of attorney that He has given to us. When we speak in His name, it is as if He has spoken it. We usually do not doubt that we are allowed to do this; however, we do doubt the authority of our own words. Therefore, if we can understand that it is not really us that has spoken it but the name of Jesus that has done it, we do not worry about the result.

We see that as we take authority in Jesus's name, the chain is on the other foot. Instead of the enemy binding us in chains, he's the one in chains. That's how it should be. Like David with the slingshot against Goliath, he knew the power of the name of God (1 Sam. 17:45). The Israelites were like children fearing a bully. They knew that Jehovah was their God but were not walking in the power and authority that they had as His children. We may feel little when the enemy attacks, but David was little too.

God has willed everything to us. Every blessing, all protection, and every good thing are ours. We are the children of the King and, that being the case, are confident that we are well taken care of as His children. We should carry ourselves with confidence. King's kids know that their Daddy takes care of them and protects them. Natural kings have guards to protect their children. God sends His angels to protect us. Once we firmly have this in our minds, we have the assurance that "There shall no evil befall thee, neither shall any plague come nigh thy dwelling" (Ps. 91:10).

When I first started getting words of knowledge, I could tell they were God's words because I could feel the anointing upon me. But I wondered why I felt the anointing when I got a word from God in church and not when God spoke to me in my prayer closet. When I asked God about this, the answer was so simple. When we are with God, talking to Him in prayer, it is an intimate time where we are talking *to* each other, communicating with each other. We are talking as one friend to another When we are in church, we feel the anointing because we are not just talking *to* God, we are talking *for* God, giving people the word God has for them.

That's the difference. I found that when the anointing is upon me it gives me the boldness and courage I need to speak that word. I don't need that boldness in my prayer time. The anointing energizes. When we are tuned in to God, we become more alive. An electric outlet in the wall is a source of electricity. A lamp needs to be plugged into the outlet in order for it to work; otherwise, it is not useful. It needs to be connected to the source of power. In order for us to be useful to God, we need to be plugged in to Him. We then feel more alive, for then we are not a separate entity, but one—we're connected to our power source, the Holy Spirit.

Sometimes people are afraid of feeling the anointing. But God will "adjust the voltage" to what the person can or is able to receive. We don't control this power. God alone takes care of it. He only gives us what we can handle.

I started becoming more confident to know that when I speak God's written Word, it is God and therefore it has the authority for miracles too. When we pray for people and get a word of knowledge for them, we can also pray God's written Word over them. It is a double whammy to the enemy!

In the chapter on responsibility, we will discuss how the enemy hits you twice, first with fear and then with guilt. He may have double punches, but so do we! As we grow in spiritual maturity, more and more is revealed and revelation increases faith. It could be as a rhema revelation of scripture or a word of knowledge revelation. It is the power that ignites faith—faith fuel!

The most amazing thing about revelation is that God gives us revelation as to what needs to be revealed to us and in our lives! That's so that we know what to ask for revelation in! This is deep, but it's like when we delve into God's Word—He will unveil revelation about that Word, almost like when we play Clue or Charades.

We are like detectives looking deeper to find the answers. God can give us spiritual revelation and directional revelation. He gives us spiritual revelation in understanding and directional revelation in mapping out His plans for us. So, spiritual revelation can lead to directional revelation and vice versa. As we go deeper in understanding God's Word and recognizing His voice, then He can lead us along the best pathways, the best direction, for our lives.

Isaiah 30:21 came to mind. It says, "And thine ears shall hear a word behind thee, saying, This is the way, walk ye in it; when ye turn to the right hand, and when ye turn to the left." Revelation releases God's promises!

3

THREE R'S

RESPONSIBILITY, RESPONSIBILITY, RESPONSIBILITY

God gives everyone special gifts. It is not just the one or two who speak in church. God speaks to everyone. He speaks *to* us personally and He speaks *through* us under the anointing of the Holy Spirit. God is the One who has given us gifts, talents, and abilities. We had nothing to do on our part for them; our part has to do with responsibility.

Part of our responsibility is spending time with God and getting to know Him. We need to spend time with Him every day. Many times, we want the gifts without taking the time to know the Giver. So many people go to church and want to know God more, but they don't know how to know Him. How does anyone get to know more about someone? It is by spending more time with them. Time is more valuable than gold and can be just as hard to find. There is more and more clutter in our lives, more and more things to do, and more and more ways to fill our time. As a result, God gets put on the back burner.

Even when a bit of time frees up, we're too tired to seek God. We have just enough energy to sit in front of the TV. That has become our instructor instead of the Holy Spirit. God is sought last, after all the other things to do. So when it comes time to seek Him, it's already the end of the day and we are too tired. We are empty and drained. It is at those times when we need the Word of God more than ever. God's Words are sweet to our spirits. They are warm and good and are nourishing and give strength to our souls. The expression "Eat my words" is generally used negatively. However, we need to eat God's Words—let them sink into our very beings, for His Words are life. Then we can speak His Word over every situation and over others, for they bring healing and success to all flesh (Prov. 4:20–22). We feed ourselves on the Word so that we can feed others. Nothing can come from an empty vessel.

When I hear from the Lord, I always feel closer to Him. It makes me feel special and privileged. Children who feel special and loved will not stray or be rebellious. God wants all His children to feel that way. But to feel that special love, they need to connect with Him. To know His heart for them, they need to take time to be with Him and to hear Him. He has given each one special gifts. Some gifts are in the natural and some in the supernatural. Most will find their natural gifts on their own. But spiritual gifts are known and grown by connecting with the Lord.

Some people were never taught about spiritual gifts, so when they get a word from the Lord, they think in worldly terms and think they are psychic. They don't realize that God is speaking to them. Many have not connected with the Lord enough to know that prayer is a two-way setup and that He talks to them; so their spiritual gifts never grow and that special relationship with the Lord is never developed. It's the parable of the soil all over again.

Communicating with the Lord and spending time with Him cultivates the soil. Many may not want to bother, some want to on Sunday, but when Monday comes, it's forgotten. God wants all His children to feel special, but what's a parent to do? The difference with natural parents being able to make the child feel special is that they start from birth. Some of God's children start connecting with Him at an early age, but many are reborn as adults. Some are not taught about gifts or about having a personal, "we talk" relationship; and that's the difference. Natural parents work with natural senses in communicating with their children. God works in the supernatural, but being familiar with the natural affects their thinking and knowledge. He speaks to them, but they don't know it's Him. That special close relationship is then missing.

Twenty-four hours seems to be getting shorter and shorter. I have found that when I seek God first, everything else will fall into place. The day just goes better. As we give God the first part of the day, we are giving Him the first fruits of our time. We give Him the first fruits of our income, so why not our time? As the saying goes, "Time is money," and time is of great value to God. We give our tithes out of obedience—we give our time out of love.

People are overburdened. This age of information and instant messages has put more pressure on us than ever before. Instead of simplifying, it has complicated. People are on a treadmill that they can't get off, going around in circles. We are like slaves to phones and computers and technology. Like the Israelites with the Egyptians working them harder and harder, technology wants more and more, faster and faster. Instead of freeing up time, it has done the opposite. Cell phones and laptops have made it possible that every minute can be devoted to them.

More and more is expected of employees. It is out of control; a pressure cooker about to explode. Even children are caught up in a whirlwind of activity. Technology has made people want more. There was even a TV program called *I Want That!* What about simple pleasures? So much communication, so little talking! We should work hard, yes, but overwork leads to breakdown of family, values, and health—both mental and physical.

So, what can we do? A good way to start is to put value on family time, being satisfied and not trying to be a super person, nor expecting this from others. Let's not be so caught up in what we have that we lose sight of who—and Whose—we are. "Be still, and know that I am God:" Psalms 46:10 says.

So often we are so busy that we do not receive God's signals, His words. It is as if our receptors are malfunctioning. We are so overstimulated by the world and are too tired to be refreshed by connecting with God. Our nerves are shot. God can soothe nerves, but we are too frazzled to be with Him. Instead, we stare at the "boob tube" to destress and refresh, but even then, we turn the channel to junk food! We have become malnourished, deadened to anything spiritual. What can we do? How do we get to that point of wanting to break the cycle of overwork, TV, work? When someone is hungry, a taste of steak or a bit of honey makes him or her want more. God's word is meat, and His word is sweet. It is soothing to sore nerves. Once we hear the Lord, we want more. Even just changing the channel to Christian programming will build strength and refresh. It's just a small change that will start to tune us in to hearing from the Lord.

There was a time when, although I was praying every day, I was spending more time lifting up my needs rather than just being with the Lord. Then one day, I felt God say that He has been waiting for me to put aside the cares and things of this world and just be with Him. He told me to sit with Him and that He missed me.

Then as I asked what was on His heart, I saw a teardrop. He was showing me that His people are too busy for Him. He longs for them, but they're too busy. I remarked that even though I spent time in prayer, how easy it is to be caught up with life's problems. I asked forgiveness for spending the time in prayer only seeking for my own needs to be met instead of spending that time getting to know Him more.

As He took me in His arms, He explained how He yearns for people to know Him intimately. His heart cries out to them. He wants that intimacy, but the world has become too complicated. There are very few simple pleasures that satisfy. He loves us. He desires us to *be* with Him more than *do* for Him. Sometimes the doing is to avoid being with Him. Sometimes, people are afraid to be with Him—of intimacy—and doing is their excuse. But He says to these ones, His arms are open. He loves them. They should not be afraid. He will not condemn them or scold them. He wants their love and their time, the most precious gifts they can give Him. He wants just a few minutes of our being with Him. He longs for His people. His arms are open. Will you come?

God enjoys our company. He likes being with us. He is the Lover of our souls, and just like lovers, He wants to be able to be with us and relax—not having to always talk about deep things, not always having to instruct us, but instead having intimacy with us.

Love builds more faith than instruction. When we realize God's love for us, we also know His care of us. Teaching and instruction are both good, but intimacy is better. We need both. Intimacy refreshes the tired soul. It renews it and fills our tank to do the instructions. Otherwise, we start running on empty. That's why God gave us a day of rest. The secret of closeness is being able to be in each other's presence without saying a word and being comfortable. It's also about being able to talk about our dreams for the future. Isn't that what it's like with our spouses? I think that Jesus must feel the same way and wants to be with us sometimes just like on a date.

God was teaching me about all this when He showed me that we are so congested with having to do so many things, it was like being in a traffic jam. The congestion in people causes them to remain where they are. It prevents them from moving forward in the Lord. Is it any wonder why we haven't reached our destination? We just can't seem to get where we are going. What should we do?

As we turn our hearts and thoughts to God, even throughout the day, it trains our spirits to be tuned in to Him and to hear Him, wherever we are. We learn to walk in the Spirit at the same time as when we have to do things in the flesh. But time with the Lord in the still moments is even more special to Him. We talk to our husbands during the day as we are doing other things, but special moments come as we take time to be alone and focus on each other. It's a time of renewal between the two of you.

Each day, taking some time with the Lord alone, not doing other things, renews our spirits and draws us closer to Him; we reconnect. When people are so congested with doing, they can't fit God in. The ironic thing is that they are congested because of time schedules, yet if they make time for the Lord, He will put everything in its proper time and place. Things just seem to fit in better. And then the traffic jam and congestion will start moving again, for only He can get us to our destination. It's by giving God the time we don't think we have to give that we get what we need. Remember the widow and her son? She gave Elijah the last cake (1 Kings 17:11–16). The barrel never emptied. Put God in the congestion, and He will direct the traffic and get us moving again.

Is there a solution when time is at such a premium? I believe that just as giving our tithe is proportionate to the amount of money we have, so is our time. We may not have two or three hours to spend each day in prayer, but we can give what we have. If we can only get up fifteen minutes earlier each day, then do that. It is our desire to be with God that matters. That is how we grow in the knowledge of Him—time. It is the time being with Him, not doing for Him. Sometimes the people who do the most works for God, know Him the least. Never neglect the *be* to do. When we do this, we become weak and ineffective. It is the Mary-Martha thing.

We all need to do but not at the expense of not being in God's presence. God's presence is what gives us the strength to do. Only doing and not being will wear us out. Balance is the key. All Martha means we are doing for the Lord but not learning from Him—all work, no presence. But Mary also needs to share what she's learned with others. Mary has heart knowledge from being in God's presence; Martha has head knowledge from what she's learned about the Lord from others. Martha performs needed services; Mary soaks up God's presence. Both are necessary, but one without the other is out of balance. Presence should come first then programs.

I think that one of the enemy's deceptions is that if he can get you to do (by making you feel guilty if you don't) and not be, then you're so busy doing that it prevents you from connecting with the Lord. This is true even if we're doing good things. Sometimes, we need to take a break from worldly things and just rest in His presence.

One of the hardest things to learn is that we cannot be all things to all people. That's God's job, not ours. It is a sign of maturity when we realize this, for Satan comes as light. And if he can get you to try to be all things, even good things, he can wear you out by doing and thereby take you away from God's purpose and plan. We can be so busy at times running to and fro, we are like chickens with our heads cut off. God's destiny will never have time to be worked out. It's doing instead of being, taken to a new dimension. That's why it's so important to be hearing God.

Don't let people put things on you that is not of God, for only the one who hears God's instructions walks in what He has for them.

Sometimes, it means being out of step with the crowd. Sometimes, it means doing the opposite of what everyone else is doing. It's so easy to think that you are doing something for God when you're really just going along with the crowd, doing what the people think you should do. If you want to know what God wants you to do, spend time with Him and ask Him! God's Word says in Isaiah 55:8, "For my thoughts are not your thoughts, neither are your ways my ways, saith the Lord." To know God's thoughts means spending time with Him and asking Him. One of the enemy's tricks is to get you to feel guilty when you don't do what the rest of the crowd is doing because it's "for the Lord." But God didn't call us to fit in; He made each of us individually for His purpose and plan.

We as Christians have so much trouble saying no. I've learned that it's OK for us to set boundaries and limits on our time. There are always those who will wear us down and sap our energy and strength so that we are not able to do the assignment God has for us. I am not talking here about helping those people with a need for the moment and can't help himself or herself, a person who truly appreciates your help. I'm talking about the "me" people who want people to do for them what they can do for themselves. If we're not careful, they will get us off track for what God would have us do. They are like suckers on a young tree—they prevent growth.

We are to help those who are humble, those who help others as they can. They may be down for the moment but will do everything they can to help themselves and then give back and help others as soon as they get back on their feet. Washing each other's feet is serving one another, but being the mat they walk on is another story.

Growing always comes with a price. In this case, the price is time. It is taking the time to listen to God, getting to know His character and becoming more like Him. How can we know God and become more like Him when no time is spent with Him? If we are not growing in the Lord, becoming more like Him, then how are we growing and in which direction are we going? Growing in the gifts has to be right alongside growing in character and becoming more Christlike. Time with God is the key—knowing God, talking with Him, and hearing *from* Him, not just about Him.

We need to understand that if we want spiritual gifts, it takes responsibility on our end. There are those who are feeders—they receive God's word and feed others. And there are also those who just want to be fed. Many are afraid of the responsibility, afraid of making a mistake, or just don't want to bother. They are looking to someone else for a word. However, they have a responsibility too. People that are moving in the spiritual gifts need to be responsible to speak that which God has given them. It takes courage. People on the receiving end of a word need to be responsible too.

When God does a miracle and answers their prayers, they need to have the courage and the responsibility to testify and thank God publicly for the blessing that they have received—even when fear comes upon them. They have to give God glory when He blesses them and to not be afraid of the enemy (and the fear he tries to put in them). It takes courage to speak what God says, and it takes courage to thank Him publicly. In its simplest form, God does not put fear on us; Satan does that. So are we going to obey God or the enemy? We say we would never obey the enemy, but isn't that what we do when we give in to fear and not speak the word or not give God the glory when we are healed? One way the enemy gets us to fear and not give God glory when we are healed is that he tells us that if we speak about our healing, we will lose it.

I believe this spirit of fear is a stronghold that prevents people from giving God glory and thereby perpetuating the lie. But things of the spirit are opposite things of the flesh. Testimony will expose this fear as a lie and keep the very thing that they are afraid of losing (their healing) from happening. We should take a lesson from Job. The very thing he was afraid of happened (Job 3:25).

Although faith and fear are opposites, they often go hand in hand. For when the enemy puts fear in us, faith has to step in to fight it. In war, the bravest soldiers fear. It's not that bravery means no fear: it means that fear doesn't stop them from doing what they are required to do. When I talk about fear in this chapter, it is not the natural emotion that is in us to protect us that I am talking about. It is not the fear that we have to protect us from danger. I'm talking about the spiritual fear that the enemy puts on us to prevent us from doing what God has told us to do or the worry he puts on us to get us to doubt what God told us He would do for us.

When this spiritual fear comes in, it is faith that we need to fight it, trusting God to help us win the battle. It is not fear that determines whether or not you failed. All people fear. It's how you handle it. It is a lifelong, day-to-day battle. Satan will not just put fear on you one time, and then it never comes back. And many times, after the enemy hits us with fear, he hits us again with guilt for having feared.

As a child, I remember a toy that was a "Punch and Judy" toy. You would hit it and it would go to the ground and then bounce back up so that you could hit it again. I think that's how Satan works. If the first shot of fear doesn't get you down, he tries again with guilt. However, when you grow in God, you learn to fight fear with faith. As you grow in spiritual maturity, it becomes easier each time the attack comes. Heroes are not people who have no fear; they just overcome it. Each day, we overcome as our faith gets stronger. Fear is not failure! Letting it stop you from obeying God is. Giving in to fear and then giving up is the only way you can fail. It takes more faith to believe and press in to God when fear comes in than when all is going well.

God gave me an analogy one time to help me to press through the fear. He gives me these analogies because He knows I will remember them. He showed me a beehive and then told me that sometimes we have to fight the bees to get to the honey. But He also reassured me that when He's with me I will not get stung. Good things are always worth fighting for. The enemy doesn't want us to have good spiritual gifts, so he puts up a fight. We have much better weapons than he does—Jesus's name and God's Word. Therefore, we should not be afraid to go for the honey.

Responsibility is a two-way street. We speak the word God gives us, and in turn, the one who receives the word gives back to God by giving Him glory for what He has done. God is always merciful and He wants to bless us. But I believe God favors those who are obedient, thankful, and responsible with the blessings He bestows on them. Sow thankfulness and reap blessings!

We are responsible for everything God gives us. Some people will take care of their own things but do not take as much care with other's things as they do their own. For example, how many times have we stayed at a hotel and noticed scratched furniture? How many of us have rented a furnished apartment only to discover that the previous renter did not take good care of the furniture? Everything is the Lord's, and we should care for it as such as what we learn in the Word: "The earth is the Lord's and the fulness thereof; the world, and they that dwell therein" (Ps. 24:1).

We're just "renting"; everything is God's. How we take care of our worldly possessions and gifts determines how we take care of our supernatural gifts. Are we responsible enough to value what God gives us even if we're just renting them? When God gives us a word for someone, how do we take care of it? Are we responsible? When we borrow something, we should return it in the same condition we received it. If everything belongs to God, this is especially true. If we are responsible with little, God can trust us to be responsible with much. When He gives a word, if we're responsible, He will give us more. God uses us when He knows He can trust us with what He gives us. He will continue to use us as we are faithful to say what He tells us to say and do what He tells us to do.

With responsibility comes humility. It may seem that courage and humility are contradictory; it is not. It takes courage to step out in faith, even though you may look foolish if you've missed it and heard wrong. Walking in humility means that bringing God's word to someone in need is more important than your pride, so you're not afraid if people see you've made a mistake. It means putting your needs aside and yielding to the Holy Spirit so that you can hear for another.

I find that during praise and worship, as I am under the anointing and yielding to the Holy Spirit, my needs are the furthest thing from my mind. In fact, I could get a healing word for someone in my family and don't even think of them when I get it. It may take several days before I make the connection and realize that I could have claimed that healing for them. God will usually remind me of the word He gave me as I pray for them in my daily prayers. That is how disconnected I am to myself at those times. If there are times when I cannot disconnect from my problem or need, I will usually not get a word. Or if I do, I have to make sure it is not my flesh. We have to be so responsible at these times. How often have we listened to someone giving a word and knew it had to do with what they were going through at the time? We then have to wonder if the word was just a personal word for them or their wishful thinking. We must put our problems and needs last.

Responsibility also means trusting God, even when the word doesn't make sense to you and you're still speaking it. So often I will get a word that means nothing to me but is exactly the phrase a person has been praying about or feeling in their heart. For example, one time, God gave me the specific words *shattered dreams*. It made no sense to me but was exactly what someone was feeling, and God will eventually bring her dream to pass. He wanted her to know not to give up on that promise. If I would have gone by my own thinking or reasoning, I may not have said it using those exact words, and God would not have been able to comfort this person.

Sometimes, God will give you a name of someone you don't know. You have to step out in faith and speak it. When this first happened to me, I did not understand why I would get a name, especially if it wasn't someone who was in church. I started to realize very quickly that sometimes the person has no other way of hearing God, except for a person who is a friend or relative who is in church and can relay the message. Sometimes, it is also a way that God will let the person praying for them know that He has heard their prayers.

To give you an example of this, one time, God gave me a name of someone I knew did not go to our church. In fact, I had no knowledge of anyone with that name, for it was not a common name. I spoke it, and a lady in church said that she had been praying for this person and in fact had spoken to this person the night before. The word I had gotten for this person (in addition to the name) was that God wanted to heal her. The lady in church said this person told her the night before that she was giving up believing God for her healing! God is so good and cares so much for His children. All He needs is a willing vessel. Are you willing to take the risk?

To summarize, there are many facets of responsibility when dealing with spiritual gifts.

Why don't more people walk in the gifts God gives them? These are some of the reasons:

- Some people don't know it is God who is speaking to them; they think it's their own mind and thoughts.
- Some would rather be fed than be feeders.
- It takes time in prayer—a relationship—for in order to give out, you need to be filled up to have something to give.
- A compassion for others is needed to be able to stop thinking about our needs so that we can be open to hear what God wants to speak to us about another's needs.
- It takes a combination of courage and being humble. It takes courage to step out in faith even though we may look foolish if we make a mistake. It means that bringing God's word to someone in need is more important than our pride. It means trusting God, even when the word does not make sense to us.
- Our character should equal our level of anointing or gifting.
- We need to remain obedient. Use it or lose it. If God gives you a word and you don't speak it, He'll find someone who will. This does not mean He will not give you other chances to speak, especially if you usually do step out and are obedient at other times. I can remember several times when I got a word of healing for someone and did not speak it because I thought it was just my flesh and God had someone else speak that same word. Sure enough, the person needing that healing came up for prayer. This is not just for words of healing. One time, I got a scripture verse—"Come unto me, all ye that labour and are heavy laden, and I will give you rest" (Matt. 11:28). I didn't say it, and then during intermission, a lady gave the pastor a note saying she felt God was telling her that someone was

feeling pain and sorrow. God uses those who are willing to take the risk and speak it, even if they are humbled. God does not need us, for He can make the rocks speak. So, with you or without you, His word will come forth.

- God gives us the desire to be used as His vessel. Which came first, the chicken or the egg? The desire or the gift? When God gives us the gift, He also gives us the desire to be used in that particular gifting.

The bottom line is this: when God gives us a word, it is our responsibility to speak it or to pray for it, whichever God tells us. Only then will we have done our part, what we are responsible for. Our job is to deliver the word God gives to us; God's job is to do the rest. We speak what the Holy Spirit tells us to say, and then we leave it in the Lord's hands. We are also not responsible for whether or not the person receives it. Once they hear the word, then it is their choice as to what they do with it. They have to be open to receive. As God's vessel, there will be times when God gives us a word and the person does not want to hear it or accept it. We may know it's from the Lord, and we will have to know how to deal with this. We should not be hurt, for it has nothing to do with us. We just give it to the Lord and keep going. When they do not receive the word, they are not rejecting us; they are rejecting the word.

We are also not responsible for the result of the word—for example, whether people are healed. That part has nothing to do with what we do. We give the word to the person, and the Holy Spirit takes over from there. When I first started getting words of knowledge, I struggled when I got a healing word, and nothing happened right away. I would keep praying, thinking that maybe I did not pray good enough or long enough or used the right words.

I then realized that by thinking this way, I was actually thinking that I had something to do with it. I did not think this way intentionally, but this being new to me, I thought I must not be praying well enough and would feel guilty, like I let God down! But God showed me that when He gives a word, people don't even have to be prayed for to receive it. Faith comes by hearing and hearing by the word of God (Rom. 10:17). In fact, many times, people are healed as they hear the word before anyone else does anything else. And so often, there can be several people who, when a word is given, believe that word is for them and are healed at the same time. His anointing breaks the yoke. It is His anointing; His Holy Spirit that does it and not the words we use.

As we grow, we learn above all things that it's not what we say, it's not how we pray, but it's the Holy Spirit working through us. Even if we prayed in a language that the person did not understand, they would still be healed. Therefore, it's not what we say or what we pray. We do not have to prove that we can pray the right way, for God is the one who does it. And if it is God who does it—and He does—then the credibility rests on Him. It is up to the Lord. We do not have to prove that it is God; He can do that Himself! We just need to be ourselves. God made us the way we are and He loves us just that way. We just need to relax, let God use us as His vessels, and we'll see His mighty power working in us. This revelation lifted such a burden from me.

KNOW WHEN TO HOLD 'EM AND WHEN YOU SHOULD HAVE TOLD 'EM

One morning, as I was getting some things done in the house, I was asking God for wisdom to know what to do with what He tells me. I got the impression that God was saying that that is the right question to ask wisdom for. The question isn't that God will tell us things; the question is, what we should do with what He tells us!

Responsibility is also being able to be trusted to keep a secret. Just as it takes responsibility to speak the words God gives us, it also takes responsibility to know when God is telling us not to speak them or to know to wait until He tells us to speak them. A friend may take you into their confidence and tell you something and they expect you to keep what they've told you to yourself. God is our friend, and He shares secrets with us. They are for our ears only. He needs to be able to trust us with what He tells us in the secret things.

Sometimes, God tells us secret things in our own lives. Sometimes, He tells us something about another. When He tells us something about someone else, it could be because He wants us to pray for this person or so that we could be more understanding of him or her. So many times, we form wrong opinions of others or judge their behavior without walking in their shoes.

God will sometimes give us a word that is for us alone to know for that moment in time. It takes wisdom and maturity to know when, how, and even whether or not we should speak it. God wants to be able to trust us with His secrets until it is His timing to reveal them. How do we know what to do? God will give us guidance as to handle it. This maturity comes with time.

We need to be sensitive to the Holy Spirit and what He is telling us to speak and not to speak as well as *how* to speak it. There are times when God will tell us something that would embarrass the person if we spoke it. For example, it could be a sensitive issue about health that needs to be spoken in terms that will not embarrass. God will tell us how to do this. Sometimes, God will tell us to wait until His timing is right to speak it. If we're not sure as to what God wants us to do, ask Him and wait until He answers.

We should not have fear about this, for God will give us baby food at first until we grow and learn how to handle the meat. We will know as we grow. Above all, it requires love to be able to put others' feelings first, just as it requires love for others for God to use us. Love is the key as well as sensitivity to the Holy Spirit.

God is so patient and kind. He understands that we are learning and that we desire to see signs and wonders and answers to prayer. We just need to understand that the only way to see these things happen is to yield to the Lord, give the word He's given us to give, and let His Holy Spirit take it from there.

Learning is never easy. There's a song that says it's not easy "being green." We should not fear the mistakes or despise the humbling. It's all a part of the growth process. As I was talking to the Lord in prayer one day, wondering when I would get it right, He gave me a large sign. I had to laugh as I read,

Have patience with me—I'm under construction!

4

PERCEPTION

WHAT YOU SEE IS WHAT YOU GET

We have learned in chapter 2 that revelation *precedes* reception. We also need to understand that perception *leads* to reception. How we perceive what is going on in different areas of our lives will affect what we receive. We first get a revelation that allows us to understand a word, and then how we will perceive it on our end will lead to what we receive.

We have to let go of past thinking so we can move into future promises. In fact, they are only future promises until we are ready to receive them.

One area in which we need perception to receive is in the area of sowing. Most people think of sowing in terms of only money. Sowing isn't always money. Praying for others is sowing also. Giving food and clothing is sowing. People who realize praying for others is sowing pray more. It is perception so that there can be reception. You can't receive unless you realize what you have given is sowing and therefore reaping comes.

People overlook these areas of giving. I never really thought of my prayers for others as sowing until Jesus showed me an apple orchard. Each tree was the fruit of a prayer; for each time we pray, our prayers bear fruit. I was wondering why there were many apples on the trees when the tree was from one prayer. I realized that it's because many people can be touched as a result of one prayer. For example, when the person for whom we prayed gets an answer, their faith is then increased and they tell others, and then these other people's faith is also increased. This produces something good—it produces fruit. Or maybe we've been praying for the salvation of a loved one, and when they come to the Lord, they then start witnessing to others and so on.

Fruit always has seeds to produce more. Apple trees are pruned regularly. They don't get too big or too tall; they produce more with being wide than with height, and they produce more with maturity. Therefore, it also means that people don't have to be prominent or well known to be productive. They just have to be mature in the love of the Lord.

I have always believed that when we pray for others, our prayers will also be answered. We reap what we sow. When we sow prayers for others, they are seeds that will reap answers for our own prayers. We don't plant an apple seed and get a peach tree. What we do for others, God will do for us.

Our prayers are not just words or sounds; they are form and substance. We are created in God's image, and just as His words take form, so do ours. In the world, it is called self-fulfilling prophecy. An encouraging word is sowing. However, a discouraging word is also sowing, so we should be careful what we sow. The problem lies not so much in what others speak over us that is undeserved—and I'm referring here to when people speak bad over us because they don't like us—for the Bible tells us that a curse without a cause shall not alight (Prov. 26:2). The problem lies in speaking negative words over ourselves.

God's Word tells us to control our tongue, for it is a powerful weapon (James 3). Just as good words sown reap blessings, negative words reap curses. A smile is sowing, and a scowl is sowing. Have you noticed that if one member of the family is in a bad mood, it's contagious? It is reaping what is being sown. Most times, we don't realize that everyday actions are sowing something. Perception is very important because it affects every area of your life. What people perceive affects the outcome in the natural. A smile begets a smile. If we don't understand this in the natural, we will not understand this in the supernatural. We won't be able to perceive things going on in their spirit. How people see things affects their lives.

We've all heard about how we see the glass, whether we see it as half empty or half full. Do we see God as a loving Father or a harsh one? Do we realize our places as sons and daughters of the King or of a pauper? Perception becomes reality to us. The deception is that people don't realize they are reaping because they don't even realize that they've sown! Therefore, they don't know to look to reap at all, especially when they've sown things like prayers.

Sometimes, people go through the motions of giving without allowing God to give back because they don't realize they can receive. Some think that it's even greedy or un-Christian. It's as if they've closed themselves to receiving like a one-way door—out but not in. They don't perceive that they can receive from what they've given, or they think that they shouldn't receive. That it is wrong. That's stinkin' thinkin'! Giving and not allowing God the joy of giving back robs Him of His pleasure. We don't give to receive, but when we give, the law of sowing and reaping goes into effect. We give and it gives us joy to help others. God gives back because it gives Him joy to bless us, especially because He knows we'll keep giving. The more we give, the more He'll give and so on. We have to perceive it to receive it.

Satan has been having a field day in this area because of wrong perception in God's children. How many natural kings' children do you see living in lack? Would that bring honor to the king? Once God's children realize who they are in Him, they can receive all that He has. Yet many of God's children are living in lack because they don't understand this. When Christians look at the cross, they know that Jesus shed His blood for their sins to be forgiven. But He also shed his blood with the crown of thorns on His forehead to break the curse of the sweat of their brow. Adam brought about the curse, but Jesus took it away. As the Bible says, "My people are destroyed for lack of knowledge:" (Hosea 4:6).

We need to know this and perceive it in our hearts so that we don't accept what the enemy puts on us. If we believe the enemy's lies, we will receive all that he has. Satan will try to get our focus off of the Lord and onto natural things by putting fear and worry in our minds about health, finances, relationships, etc. He wants to trap Christians into receiving these lies from him. God gave me an analogy one day concerning this very thing. He showed me a mousetrap and told me that Satan sets many traps, but the smart mouse never gets caught. I asked how I could be like the smart mouse. He answered by telling me to stay close to Him—walking with Him, letting Him guide me, listening to His words—and then the spring will be sprung. Don't be trapped by a little piece of cheese when God has the whole wheel for us! Wake up! King's kids don't eat crumbs.

The tendency is that when we go through a season of lack, we worry about it. When we worry about it, we give it a place of being most important. When we focus on the Lord in plenty or lack, we take the importance off money and put it on the Lord. Then, since it's not the most important thing in our life, we will give it freely, knowing that God will see to it that more will come. In the natural, when we cut off a flower bud, two will grow in its place. Spiritual law is that when we give, it will be given unto us in good measure, pressed down, shaken together, and running over (Luke 6:38). We get back more than what we've given, just like what happens to the flower in the natural. We believe this law of nature because we see it. We need to perceive this spiritual law also. We understand the nature of it. We come to perceive it as law, not theory. We see it as fact, not hope.

We are not only God's children; we are the brides of Christ. A child knows that he can ask his daddy for anything and receive it; a bride knows she already has it! Many times, we don't see our own self-worth, our value. When we can see our own worth, we can receive what God has for us. We are highly prized in His eyes, but we need to realize our own worth first in order to perceive ourselves as God sees us. He wants us to walk in the fullness of all He has for us. Don't let Satan put tags on us—failed here, wasn't good there, etc. So, we fail; no one is perfect. Jesus has put His nametag on us. He paid the price. We must be so frustrating to the Lord at times, for most of us place our value on how others see us or, even worse, we believe what the enemy tells us that because of a failure, we can't be blessed.

Most of us don't understand the difference between conviction and condemnation. Conviction comes *before* we ask forgiveness in order for us to be aware of our sin and to know to ask for forgiveness. Once we ask forgiveness, there is no need of conviction. Condemnation comes *after* we ask forgiveness, and it is the enemy who does it. It's perception again because if he can get us to feel guilty, we won't be expecting the blessings.

God doesn't expect perfection; He expects correction. God places our value on the fact of who we are in Him. He loves us just the way we are. Our self-worth should be on how He sees us. We are His bride—blood bought and washed clean, chosen and purchased by Him. Now, be His bride and receive all that goes with it. For how would it be if Ruth married Boaz and still felt she had to glean the fields for food? That would disgrace Boaz. (Read the book of Ruth.) We need to honor God by receiving all that He has for us and not accept anything less, what the enemy would have you believe. Believe God. You have to know who you are to receive all that He has. What you perceive is what you'll attract like a magnet. We have to perceive it to receive it.

What about when we give and we don't see the harvest right away? We tend to think that God hasn't noticed or maybe He has forgotten us. But God does not forget. He sees our gifts. I think that God has a spiritual bank account for each one of us, and this account gathers interest. The wait is because, if we were to "cash in" on our account right away, the gain would be small. If we wait for God's timing, the gain is what He would have for us.

We find it hard to believe that the harvest will still come because of our humanness and because it may have been such a long time that we have been waiting. However, God takes good care of our investments, and they will be given back to us—good measure, pressed down, shaken together, and running over (Luke 6:38). The difference between earthly investments and investing in God's kingdom is this: with God, there are two harvests from one seed. The harvest we receive in the natural, on earth, does not deplete our eternal bank account! It does not take away from our reward in heaven. Therefore, if we don't see the harvest in our timing, it's not because God has forgotten us. It is because the harvest has been reinvested to make more. God is the Lord of the Harvest; and we can be assured that when we receive the harvest on earth, our spiritual blessings—our spiritual bank accounts—are still waiting for us in heaven.

God takes pleasure in giving His children good gifts (Matt. 7:11; James 1:17). As we understand this, we will receive it. In the area of our talents and abilities, what and how much we perceive we have determines what and how much we will receive—perceive big, receive big. God does exceeding, abundantly more than we can imagine (Eph. 3:20). I sometimes think that if we could see ourselves the way God sees us, our lives would change, our perceptions would change, and our goals and dreams would change.

Self-esteem is a matter of perception. Those who see themselves through God's eyes have good self-esteem, and they know that they can do all things through Christ that strengthens them (Phil. 4:13). Good self-esteem is about knowing who we are in Christ. It has nothing to do with pride. It has nothing to do with greed. It has to do with confidence as God's child to receive what He has for us. Good self-esteem is about knowing that God will work out His plans for us and that they are better than what we can dream for ourselves. Good self-esteem is being humble enough to know it is by God's grace and not our own abilities, whereby we have received the blessings. It is treating others kindly and being a blessing to them. We should never forget that God blesses us in order for us to be a blessing to others. For how we treat others will determine how we are blessed, how long we'll keep the blessing, and whether or not it will multiply. When we pray, give, and look to help others, when we have a bigger heart for others than our own problems, only then will blessings overflow to us. When we have good self-esteem, we have hope in God for a good future. Hope big, dream big, and walk in everything that God has for you, knowing that what He has for you is bigger than your biggest dreams. In God, there is no end.

We also know that each person is configured differently, each has a different makeup, a different personality. God made each of us unique. As we grow to new levels in the Lord, we begin to appreciate each one for the person they are and the different gifts each one has been given. They do not have to fit into our mold or see things the way we do. We begin to see them with Jesus's eyes. We begin to look for the good in them. We remember that a person is the way they are because of something that may have happened in their life. We don't judge where they are now, for there is always a reason behind it. We don't fall into criticism but accept them. That's when we realize that God is bringing us to a new level in Him.

Criticism has to go, and when something goes, something else has to come in to fill the spot. Love will come in and fill it. Then we will not compare ourselves to anyone or anyone to us. God made each of us for a different purpose. We should also not try to be like anyone else. God made us the way we are. To be dissatisfied with the way we are is to be dissatisfied with the way God made us. He loves us the way we are. When we realize this, Jesus's light will shine from us, that love magnet that will draw not only people but blessings as well. All things are drawn to the Light.

As we grow in the gifts, we start to realize that the interpretation of the word is even harder than being tuned in to the word. It's all about communication, and we have to make sure that we don't get our flesh involved. I learned early on the importance of saying the word God gives you exactly as you get it. I usually did not get words of knowledge of healing by feeling the pain like some people do. I usually just got the actual word.

One particular Sunday, however, I felt tightness in my chest, and since I never have this, I knew that it must be God wanting to heal someone. Instead of saying it exactly as I felt it, I said that I believed God wanted to heal chest pain. No one responded. But then, someone else said that she felt God wanted to heal someone with tightness in his or her chest, and someone did respond to that word. God knows exactly what the person is feeling and the words that will relate to them in a way that they will know it is God speaking to them. I've learned to be very accurate and say exactly the words God gives me or exactly what He lets me feel.

The same word can also mean several different things. It's just as in the natural, when we speak, we can say something that can mean one thing to us and something entirely different to someone else. It's like two telegraph poles with a wire in between them to relay messages. If there's a crack in the wire, the message gets broken. We send out a message in one way, and the person receives it another way, usually as a result of past experiences. We must also not let our life experiences interpret what God is saying to someone else. A word can very often mean two different things. Isn't this true with men and women? How many times will a wife say something to her husband and he interprets what she says in an entirely different way than what she believes that she is saying! A funny story comes to mind as an example of this.

My husband and I were traveling to meet our son's future in-laws for the first time. We were also going to be stopping at our daughter's house on the way home and usually brought some treat for our granddaughters. I was thinking that we should bring a fancy dessert to our son's in-laws-to-be, and so I mentioned to my husband that we should look for a bakery. We passed a Hostess bakery, and my husband mentioned to me that we should stop there and get some cupcakes with the crème filling inside.

Mortified, I told him we could never do that. He asked why we couldn't as he was sure that they would really like them, and he said that they probably never had them before. I told him everyone has had those cupcakes and what kind of impression that would make! My husband very seriously said he felt that they would really enjoy them. When we finally realized that we were not talking about the same thing, we could not stop laughing! He was talking about bringing the cupcakes to our granddaughters, and I was talking about bringing dessert to the in-laws! All from talking about a bakery! We have since told that story to our son's in-laws and, every time we visit, say we should bring those cupcakes.

Spiritual miscommunication can be very real too. There are two ways of interpreting wrong. The first is when we are spiritually "hard of hearing." I'll give an example of this.

One time, I thought God was saying the word *verizon*. When I asked God about this—because it didn't make sense—I heard Him say "*Horizon*, horizon, not *verizon*." Eh, Lord? The second is that we can put the wrong meaning on a word. For example, I thought the word *horizon* was a name of a company that God was instructing me to contact, but I found out later that He was trying to tell me about something "on the horizon."

Both misinterpretations were dealing with something that I had been praying about, and I certainly interpreted the word incorrectly. Both miscommunications with the same word! We need to be fine-tuned so that we can interpret correctly and perceive what God is telling us. A sheet of music with one missing note changes the tune!

Another area of needing to change our perception is when we are weighed down with burdens. Before we even realize it, they become all we focus on. Then, as they become bigger and bigger, we search for a miracle from God. As I was praying for just such a miracle day after day, God started to reveal to me that even though I was in prayer to Him, my need of the miracle was becoming bigger than my need of being with Him. God wants us to search for Him—not the miracle—for we find our miracle in Him. He showed me that when He gets bigger, the need gets smaller and smaller and becomes no big thing. It gets put in its proper perspective. It's all in how we see it.

In the natural, what seems like a big burden to one is nothing to another. How often do we wonder why this one is so worried about that or that one so worried about this and think our worries are bigger? It's all in the eye of the beholder. That's the natural part. In the spiritual, nothing is too big or too burdensome for God. What seems to be so big to us in our minds regarding our personal situation is no big thing for Him. So why worry? God can handle it. Genesis 18:14 states, "Is anything too hard for the Lord?" If we could see what God sees and know what He knows, we would be at peace. As we trust the Lord and obey Him, everything moves in the Spirit to affect things in the natural. And even though God's timing may not be our timing, things usually work out if we don't lose faith. There's the test.

Will you stop believing over time? Will your faith hold up? The flesh believes what the senses tell it. The spirit believes what God tells it. That battle is one everyone will fight. What we perceive in the natural is not what is going on in the spiritual. John 16:33 tells us that in the world, we shall have tribulation, but that we should be of good cheer, for He has overcome the world.

One day, as I was coming to the Lord with a burden, I got a picture of something like silly string that children play with, all over me. God started to show me that the silly string was like the lies of the enemy tangling me up with fear and worry. Each new day, another string was added as I became bound with fear. God showed me that I needed to break out of that mind-set by realizing God's promises. As we do this, our faith replaces the fear. The enemy works gradually, putting one string on us at a time. We don't even realize it. He does this with one small worry then another and another until we have a mind-set built on his lies.

God wants us free. He wants us to have confidence in His words and promises. Satan would try to shake our confidence in God's promises, but the only thing he can do is to try to change our perception and only if we let him. He can't take away the promises that God has given us.

What we perceive is a mountain is only a molehill for God. If we were to go to the top of a mountain, we would see the land below in a different perspective. We are removed from what is going on below and see everything more clearly. Sometimes, when we're in a situation, we let it consume us to the point where it completely surrounds and engulfs us. But if we rise above it and look down upon it, we can get the proper perspective. That is why we can see the answers to other's problems more than our own.

What part do emotions play in perception? If we let our emotions control us, we may not be able to hear the Lord correctly. Fear is an example of one emotion that can block us from hearing clearly—so can anger and pride and our own wishes, to name a few. It's not that emotions are bad, but when we let them control us, then God cannot use us in the way He would like to.

God needs us to listen to His voice and not our emotions. When we are emotional, we are going by our feelings and wants and not His voice. That will not accomplish anything. How frustrating it must be to the Lord when He is trying to give us a word and we don't want to hear what He has to say because it may not be what we want to do! God has our best interests at heart. May God help us hear His voice over our own wants and emotions and obey Him.

What about when we do not feel God's love? What about when we feel sick or tired or lonely or depressed? We could be joyful one day and discouraged the next. Feelings change. God's Word says He changes not (Mal. 3:6). His love for us is always there; His Word remains the same.

As children, we love the challenge of playing games; we love to win. As we practice playing these games, we get better and better at winning. Life on earth is similar, learning how to handle its challenges. Once we learn to give the burdens (challenges) to God, it makes winning easier, and we have joy. We perceive that life is a learning game to prepare our hearts for heaven.

5

BUILDING CHARACTER

YOUR CONSCIENCE METER—
HOW DO YOU MEASURE UP?

We all want spiritual gifts, but we also need to know that our character has to measure up to our level of gifting. As we grow in the Lord, we increase in Christ-like character and credibility. This is not just putting on our "Sunday best" but being Christ-like in all we do. Our actions need to be aligned to the Word of God. When we are filled with the Holy Spirit, there is outward evidence by our words, deeds, and actions. We crucify the flesh. It takes discipline at first, but as the Holy Spirit fills us up, it becomes natural. If we don't do this, we will not walk in victory or have only partial victory. We will not walk in all God has for us because we have not given Him all of us. If we have our way, we will only give God the parts that are easy to give, parts that don't take much effort to give. The rest of us will then conform to this world.

This means our lamps are only partially full. Whatever you fill the lamp with is what it contains. Be filled with the oil of the Holy Spirit, not the junk of the world and people will see God in you. It will be what makes you different. At first, it starts with one drop at a time and then more and more until it becomes a steady stream—it is life, it is energy, it is better than vitamins.

Vitamins bring health to our physical being, but the oil of the Holy Spirit brings life and energy to both the physical and the spiritual. For as our soul prospers, so does our body; and as we are filled with the Holy Spirit's anointing, we let it overflow to others. That is the purpose. The oil that goes into the lamp is not just for the lamp itself, but it is for that lamp to bring light to others. When the oil in the lamp is full, the flame is brighter. Our desire is to keep our lamp full. Our desire is to keep it to overflowing. Humility is the key. We can either be full of ourselves or full of the Holy Spirit! As I thought of this and wanting to be careful that pride did not come in, I felt that God was saying that everyone needs to have their oil checked once in a while, especially before they move ahead to their destination.

We all have been to the supermarket, and all have been the recipients of the store making an error on our bill and charging us more for an item than the correct price. They expect that we will bring it to their attention. But what happens when they charge us less? Do we also bring it to their attention? I have gone back to the store when they have undercharged me—even a small amount—and have found that the store's reaction is that of surprise. They even look at me as if I were somewhat nuts. But shouldn't we have a good conscience? It's not the amount that should determine the reaction of the heart (conscience).

We should not be surprised when transitions and testing comes. That's how we learn and grow. If we are placed in positions of gifting and do not have the maturity to handle it, we could very easily fall. Yes, there are hurdles in the race that we have to overcome, but as we stay on course and not get off track, the rewards will come, and God will be able to use us as He intended. Our character will then equal our gifting. We will walk in humbleness, and love will cover and protect us as we move into these positions. God will be able to trust us with what He's given us. We will be ready to receive the gifts, and He will be ready to release them.

It's the same concept of how a parent is able to trust the child with the keys of the car. When the child proves he is mature enough to handle the responsibility of driving, the parent releases the keys, knowing they can trust the child with the car. We have to go through the process. We have to know what to do with what we receive.

With maturity comes wisdom. Wisdom comes from experience. Experience comes from learning life's lessons. Therefore, some will have wisdom in one area but not in others. We should be ever learning, ever growing, seeking wisdom. The trick is being open to receive God's wisdom yet closing the door to false teaching and deception. There can be two extremes. Some people close themselves up to anything new or different than what they know. Others open themselves up so that they receive anything without question and expose themselves to false teaching.

Discernment is the key. It's not as complicated as it seems. Discernment allows us to know what is coming from God and what is not. It allows us to grow and learn. It gives us God's wisdom and protects us from false teaching. How do we get discernment? By asking God! As we go through life's experiences, ask God for His wisdom and discernment. We may be surprised at what He shows us!

We will all hear three voices at some point in our lives—our own flesh, the enemy, and the Lord. As we grow, we learn to recognize whose voice belongs to who. We learn to recognize the enemy's voice and learn how to deal with it; we hear our own wishful thinking and learn to realize it; and we learn to recognize that still, small voice of the Holy Spirit. We will have had to experience all three to know them in order that we can be familiar with them and not be easily deceived. Some people can recognize each voice quickly and easily. For others, it may take more experience for them to have that discernment.

Transitions can be stressful, even good ones. However, to receive all the blessings God has for us, they are necessary. We have to keep moving to walk in all God has for us. When we stay in one place, change cannot occur. This is true in the natural as well as in the spiritual. Spiritual growth means changes in character and ways of thinking that lead to maturity. Natural growth has to do with changes and increases that are evident in your surroundings. They are both connected, for learning and growing in our character will determine growth in our surroundings. It is said that attitude will affect altitude. This is true in the spirit also, for the fruit of the Holy Spirit will give us success in dealing with everyday life.

We all know people with bad attitudes who haven't gotten very far on the success meter. My grandmother used to like the old saying "You catch more flies with honey than with vinegar." We see this is very true because when we show kindness, it begets kindness. It's the golden rule—do unto others as you would have them do unto you (Matt. 7:12). This leads us to the scripture about giving: "Give and it shall be given unto you;" (Luke 6:38).

Do we see the cycle? These things are all connected. Spiritual principles will lead to natural resources. Therefore, if our character grows in spiritual principles, we will also grow in the natural. We should never fear transition and never stay in the same place in our spiritual growth. We should never assume "we've arrived." Once we stop growing, it's death. That is why when some retire, if they have nothing to transition to, they start the downward spiral. Growth is life, and our character changes as we grow in maturity. If we are stuck in our minds in one place, how can God lead us to the level of gifting He wants for us?

Testing protects us from pride, for otherwise we could easily fall. When seeds are placed in the ground, they germinate in darkness. As they get strong, they then burst forth into light and are brought into maturity. Not every seed makes it; only those who press toward the light do. It is the same in the spiritual too. We have to be brought to maturity in the spirit, for otherwise pride may come in. Many people fear making a mistake; however, that's not the issue. As much as people try not to make mistakes, everyone does, especially as they are learning. God already knows what you're going to say before we say it (Ps. 139). He doesn't expect us to be perfect; He expects us to do everything to the best of our ability. Our faithfulness is all He asks. He cannot use someone if they are not willing to step out when they sense God is speaking. Stepping out is more important than whether or not we make a mistake. It's in pride that the danger lies.

We need maturity to handle what God gives us, whether natural gifts or supernatural gifts. We need to die to self. Every good and perfect gift comes from God (James 1:17). Once the seed dies, it can sprout. Once the person dies to flesh and yields to God, they can grow. It's very easy for people to think that just because God works through them, they have a part in it or they are special. Remember, God doesn't need anyone—He can make the rocks speak! Those who look to God and not themselves are the ones whom God can trust and use.

Many times, even Christians don't realize that God is speaking to them and give credit to themselves saying they are psychic. When this happens, it is because of lack of knowledge. However, when they know better, if they give credit to themselves, it is pride. Pride enters slowly before it is recognized. Satan is patient and will put thoughts of pride in so gradually, it's not even seen until it becomes a problem. Therefore, humility and maturity are to be guarded and prized.

Those who are truly concerned that they will not become proud usually will not. They look out for it and rebuke it if it rears its ugly head. It's important to understand, then, that just as the enemy can put his thoughts in your mind with other things, he can put prideful thoughts in also. Just as we know a bad thought is not our own because it's something we would never want to happen, so it is with prideful thoughts for those who do not want them either. Our spirits are at war with our flesh. This is not unusual—it's a fact (Rom. 7:15–25). And Satan puts these very things in your mind that you fear. So, it's two against one. The flesh is at war with your spirit and Satan is at war with you too! That's the way it is.

Therefore, just as you know the bad thoughts aren't yours (why would you want something you fear?), so it is with pride. You don't want it, so it stands to reason that because you don't want these prideful thoughts in your mind, it's the enemy or your flesh that put it there. Just as we don't claim bad thoughts, don't claim the prideful thoughts that try to come in either. Rebuke them. It's the enemy's tactic to put in a prideful thought and then get you to claim it as your doing. And when you do, he puts in guilt and condemnation. Even if it's your flesh, you don't have to accept it. Just let your spirit reign and rebuke it. That's all you have to do. You are not responsible for the temptation unless you act on it. There will always be thoughts of the flesh and thoughts from the enemy. Character does not mean you don't have those thoughts. Character is when your heart tells you what's right and you act upon what your heart tells you.

When you fear pride, it's a good indication that it's not you. I still pray that people do not see me but see God. I don't want people looking to me or recognizing me in any way. I was really struggling with this as I wanted to make sure people gave God the glory. It made me very uncomfortable when someone thanked me for the word. It wasn't me! I would tell them to thank God, not me. I realized that some were just thanking me for my obedience in giving the word. I could understand that, even though it still made me uncomfortable.

But then God showed me that it doesn't have anything to do with what people think; it matters what is in my heart. I'm not responsible for what they think, but I am responsible for myself. I am responsible just to remain humble and to continue to let those who seem to look to me for a word know that it is not me but the Lord. Since I could see this on such a small scale, I can't even begin to imagine what pastors and evangelists must go through when people start thinking that they have anything to do with it. Humility is so important. It is protection.

The person who walks in pride walks in arrogance, and they don't want to change. They put themselves above all else. These people do not fear pride—they welcome it. You don't welcome something you fear. We all fall short, but those who think they don't are in for a big fall. They have lifted themselves up so high that they have a greater height to fall from. The height you lift yourself up to determines how far you fall. But those who are humble can't fall very far. As long as you take the pride dart out as soon as it enters and throw it to the ground, it's OK.

It's when you keep these darts in you—when you don't realize that they are there—that can be dangerous. When we realize pride and humble ourselves, that's when pride is defeated. Just be tuned in to the Holy Spirit and be aware so that the enemy can't sneak in. At first, he may use a very tiny dart that you don't even notice, like a tranquilizer dart to numb you for the next one that's a little larger until you don't realize it at all. We think we're doing so great that we don't always see our faults. Be aware of every little prick of pride.

Let the Holy Spirit help you sense it. He will point it out to you. Be sensitive to the Holy Spirit and rebuke the pride dart and throw it to the ground. This is called warring, doing battle, between the flesh and the spirit and between the enemy and you.

Remember, these battles are for good; they make you stronger and draw you closer to God. These battles are not for naught, for what the enemy put upon you to separate you from God will actually draw you closer as you fight. It's *how* you handle pride coming in that matters, not the prideful thought itself. Even failures can be like checks in our spirits. God can turn them for good in that He brings the failures to your attention so that you can humble yourself and ask forgiveness. That's when God can bring you to a new level in Him.

The enemy will put thoughts in our minds to get us to change our mind-set and to fear, and when these thoughts come in, they are usually accompanied with confusion. We should not fear when these thoughts come in because God knows where they have come from. However, it's important that *we* recognize where they come from also. These thoughts are usually foolish thoughts, and if we can learn to recognize these foolish thoughts right away, our enemy has lost the battle. A good way to remember about foolish thoughts is with the word *fool*:

Full

Of

Outright

Lies!

Satan will also put these foolish thoughts in our minds to get us to feel guilty and to make us feel that we are not worthy for what God has for us. He tries to get us to doubt that God will bless us or be able to use us. We need to realize that God has already given us gifts. He scheduled each day before we were born, as said in Psalm 139.

These thoughts from the enemy will not change God's plans for us; therefore, the thought is moot. Satan has nothing to do with the blessing or the gift. He just wants us to fear so that we reject being blessed or that we will wonder if we can still be used by God because we are not certain that God would still want to bless us! Since God is the giver of every good and perfect gift (James 1:17), when we realize this and that God has given it to us before time began, we understand that there's nothing that he can do to stop these blessings and we've won the battle! So, all we have to do when these thoughts that we don't want from the enemy come in, is to reject his thoughts and accept God's blessings!

When talking about character, we must also realize the fine line, the distinction between knowing we are King's kids and expecting God's best for us and selfishness. King's kids receive God's blessings and walk in the knowledge that as His children; we receive all that He has for us. He wants to bless us, but we have been given these blessings so we can use them to bless others. We do not walk in self-ishness or snobbery but with the heart of God, being kind and giving to others as God has given to us. We are to be like Jesus, not expect-ing others to wait on us or to serve us but to be like Jesus who served others. Yes, we expect God's blessings, but we don't "deserve" any-thing. It's because of His mercy and goodness to us that He blesses. Therefore, if we have God's heart, we have His mercy and goodness toward others.

As King's kids, to expect others to serve us is an abomination, since Jesus is our example and He served others. Yes, God wants us to enjoy good things, but He wants us to be a blessing to others too. Someone who is blessed yet takes and takes advantage does not have the heart of God. Their *me* is bigger than *He*. Christians are repre-sentatives of Jesus, so how does that make Him look when they take advantage of another? A "gimme" or "me" attitude is not Christian. It is worldly. All the Bible studies in the world will only give book knowledge. It is the heart that speaks and directs the walk. Can you walk the talk? Faith without works is dead (James 2:17).

Christians serve but they serve one another, not one serving *the* other. It's a two-way street. Otherwise, it's being a slave, not a server! "Therefore, all things whatsoever ye would that men should do to you, do ye even so to them:" (Matthew 7:12). Help and encourage one another. We can talk about how Christians ought to be, but do we do what we say? I woke up one night with this thought: a cow isn't valued for its moo but for the quality of the milk it produces. A cow doesn't stand out from the others by the way it moos. Do we walk the talk? What fruit are we producing?

No one wants to think about mistakes, but no one is perfect. In fact, when we recognize our failures, it is a sign of growth. We become more aware of them as we grow closer to the Lord. If we don't recognize our failures, we can't grow. Each time we are about to go to a new level, we usually will be more attuned to our shortcomings and we learn how to recognize them so we will not repeat them. It is nothing to fear. Those who fear doing anything of the flesh or that which is false will never do them intentionally.

Mistakes are unintentional and unplanned. Doing something falsely is doing it knowingly, and it's planned. Fear can be twofold. Healthy fear is the kind that keeps you from doing what is wrong. Unhealthy fear is from the enemy and it prevents you from moving into what God has for you. It is fear of making mistakes or fear that you may have made a mistake. It comes to torment you with guilt and condemnation. It is fear that God is angry with you. However, once the enemy's tactics are exposed, it's like grease on his hands and he slips away. We should never be afraid to come to the Lord with our fears, for He knows what we're feeling.

When we come to Him, He helps us to deal with it. Coming to Him in these circumstances actually pleases Him. He does not look at the fear but at the finish, the result. When we come to Him and are able to learn, the enemy gets the boot again. How much easier would it be if we could grow by having successes all the time instead of failures! But there can be no success without failure of some kind. If everyone succeeded all the time, there would be no journey, no sense of accomplishment. It's that way when we are growing too. Trials and failures make the achievement sweeter. How can we know the joy of being free from fear without ever having feared?

As we learn about handling fear, we're also learning about God. With that knowledge, our character changes to be more like Him, and we get victory over fear. So, even in these things—mistakes, failures, shortcomings—God turns everything for good and we've just taken another step toward Him. The enemy would try to put guilt and condemnation in because we've failed, but God is pleased at the result from that shortcoming because we've learned and overcame it!

Sometimes, when God starts to use us in a new area, after we take our step of faith and speak the word God gave us, the enemy will come against us with doubts and fears. He will come in after the anointing has left to bring in doubt and confusion. Was that really God we heard from?

Just like he said to Eve in the garden, his tactics remain the same. He wants to shut us up, to stop us, so that we don't allow God to use us. Press forward and tell the devil he is a liar. Don't fall into his trap. We felt it was the Lord giving us the word in our spirits; therefore, we should not let the enemy use this weapon of deception against us. Look to the Lord; for as a child learning to take his first steps, He says "Come, keep moving forward." Keep your eyes on the Lord and not on your feet; and like Peter on the water, as long as our eyes are on Him, we will have the victory. It's always a step of faith to be used in a new area. We will usually be met with resistance. But each time, we will get stronger and more confident if we don't give up when the attacks come.

I think that it must sadden God when this unhealthy fear controls and prevents people from taking steps forward. It must also show God that we don't trust Him to know our heart, that He knows we are but dust and make mistakes, and that we don't know how much He loves us. Why do we believe the enemy's lies of God being mad at us and receive his fear, guilt, and condemnation rather than receive God's love and His understanding? Satan tries to weigh us down with guilt from past mistakes. Jesus has given us freedom from condemnation on the cross. Don't let Satan nullify it by guilt when you've confessed and repented. God says to us, "Get up and try again."

God was dealing with me about this one time not too long ago. I was wondering why I make mistakes, and I felt like a failure. I was surprised when God asked me why I place more importance on my failures than on my successes. I answered by saying that I guess it was human nature. His response was that His nature is just the opposite.

He celebrates each step of faith. And if we fail, as we ask for forgiveness, our failure is no longer remembered (Heb. 10:17). Instead, God remembers each time we trusted Him, each time we obeyed Him, each time we spoke about Him, each time we spent time with Him, each time we opened our heart to Him, and each time we said we loved Him. His heart is filled with it all, so we shouldn't dwell on our failures for they disappear like smoke.

God's heart is a treasure box of all the special tokens of our love for Him. Just as a parent has a treasure box of their children's special moments—first step, first word—God has one too. He has our first step of faith, our first words of love, etc. Parents don't remember their child falling down; they remember their first steps to them. God wants us to have more confidence. If we make a mistake, it's OK. Parents will say to their child, "You are growing up on me." But I believe God says to His children, "You are growing up *in* Me. I celebrate you. I rejoice with gladness over you." He enjoys seeing us grow.

This is true when God gives us a vision for our future as well. We should not give up on that vision just because we've tried a few times and failed. We put so much pressure on ourselves to succeed that we take away our joy in trying. God opens the door for us, but the key is that we don't stop trying until the right door opens. There may be many doors that close, but if we keep using our key (not giving up), we will find the right one.

Satan will try to put fear of failure in us as it is the weapon he uses most because he's successful with it. Our success is because of the abilities that God has given to us; therefore, we hope in God and trust Him (Ps. 37). Successful people are most often those with the simplest minds, who don't think of why it can't be done. Thinking too long about something can be a bad thing, for then we allow fear to come in. If David had waited and thought too much about fighting Goliath, I wonder if Satan could have then put fear in, or maybe his flesh would be talking him out of it, giving him all the logical reasons why it couldn't be done.

I have found that after God gives me a vision, the longer I wait to do it, the harder it gets, until I start to reason that maybe the vision wasn't from the Lord after all. "Too smart for our own good" is not just a saying. Don't overthink—just trust God and do it! After God gives us a vision, birthing is always up to us. We can stop it by not following through. However, stopping birth once it's started is more painful than the birth itself. And long labor is more trying than getting it done.

Many of us let our grown-up image of ourselves hold us back. God sees the little child in us even though we act grown up. What would happen if we let the little child come out, if we let the excitement of the vision take us to places we've only dreamed about? We should be careful not to let this image of not being able to show our vulnerability in case we fail stop us from pursuing the vision. We're not perfect (even if we're grown up), and we should not try to protect that image so much that we fear our cover will be exposed if others see us fail.

Perfection prevents performance, if we wait for everything and us to be perfect. God loves us—our inner man—not the image we put on display for others to see. We have God's permission to fail; He'll love us anyway.

For those of us who are parents when our child was learning the alphabet, if he made a mistake, were we upset with him? How would we feel if he were too afraid to try learning it? Trying and making a mistake pleases God more than not trying at all. A child learns the alphabet by doing it over and over again. We learn by doing. It is not that we will never make a mistake, but the more we step out in faith, the fewer mistakes we will make. The saddest thing for a parent is, when their child does not try. Satan would have you remember all the things you did wrong. God wants us to remember all the things we did right. Satan would have you in filthy rags. God sees us in robes of righteousness. Look through God's eyes.

Sometimes we get so confused by the enemy that we allow him to get us to think we have done something wrong when we haven't! Stand your ground! Tell the devil he is a liar. Don't believe everything he tells you. Fight! For it is not in your perfection in doing everything right all the time that keeps us close to God. It's not what we do—it's what Jesus has done. We have to know this, especially when we fail or when we're not sure if we failed.

We have to use God's Word—our sword—to fight against the attacks that would condemn us. If we want to be used by God, we have to be prepared for the attacks and keep our sword handy. We also should not despise mistakes when they come, for they keep us humble. They may happen every so often, and we should not let them discourage us.

I think they happen to protect us from pride. Everyone looks back and sees how they could have done something differently or something better. It's called growth. That's how we learn. We did the best we could at the level we were at during that time. All God asks of us is that we do our best, that we are a willing vessel, and that we are willing to learn. Now, tell Satan to get lost and you will be free (from guilt). Jesus has given us freedom on the cross. Don't let Satan nullify it by guilt. Be free.

Another problem that can come upon us is when we want to grow in the gifts so badly (and quickly) that we can get impatient and start striving. I remember a time when I was asking God for more "knowings," more words of knowledge, etc. He told me I was like a frog or a little grasshopper that wants to jump and leap great distances. One of my favorite books as a child was a book called *Hoppie the Hopper*. It had a grasshopper that jumped through the pages as you turned them. I still have that well-worn book. Hoppie would jump without being prepared as to where he would land. God was telling me with that analogy that it would be better for me to take smaller leaps and land sure-footed on solid ground. I am learning and I should not be impatient, but that slow and steady wins the race.

It was good for me to desire these gifts, for God put them in my heart. But I needed to let go and let God grow me into maturity to bring me to the next level. It takes time for children to grow into adults. If it didn't, it would result in disaster—no maturity. I then remembered the movie *Big*. It is incredibly difficult to have an immature spirit in a mature body. When we are still young, we should be patient and we will learn.

Striving gets in God's way. Striving is like a hamster running on the exercise wheel; he's running hard but getting nowhere. Or if we push the gas pedal down to the floor when the car is in neutral and we're not going anywhere. Striving is like racing when we're in neutral. We have to learn to kick the flesh aside. We have to cut off the fat to get to the meat—we have to cut off the flesh to get to the spirit!

Flesh surgery is done with the knife of humility. We strive by working hard to pray for people. Our motives are good; we want to see them healed and delivered. But it's not us who does it. We can't work at it, for that is thinking that we have something to do with it. Men can strive and do their own things to try to make it all work, or they can ride on the river of living water to take them where they need to go. It sounds so simple—and it is simple—yet it's so hard for the flesh to do. The flesh says "We'll make it work"; the Holy Spirit says "Just let Me do what I do, and I will make it work better."

I had a good example of waiting on the Holy Spirit years ago when I was first experiencing the anointing. It was after worship when everyone at church was greeting one another. Someone came up to me and asked me to pray for a pain they were having. I did not feel the anointing that I felt during worship time, but I laid hands on the person and told them we would just wait and let the Holy Spirit do what He does and then just waited on the Lord.

I don't remember if I even said a word, but sure enough, I felt the anointing and the pain was gone! The Holy Spirit does amazing things and does so in a way that man cannot take credit for it. Let the Holy Spirit take control and see what He won't do! We just need to give it to God and yield and do what He tells us to do. Otherwise, we could think we prayed "good" enough, and then that gives us pride in thinking we did something. I always try to remember that people get healed even when they do not understand the language being prayed. It's the Holy Spirit that does it. It does not matter what words we say; we just have to be obedient to God.

The simplest, honest, most heartfelt prayer will reach God. Those who will strive will not thrive. It is a gift, not a get! You cannot strive to get it. If we seek first the Kingdom of God, then all these other things will be added unto us (Matt. 6:33).

It's important for us to know the difference between striving and performance. Striving is when we desire to hear so much that we create pressure upon ourselves and strain to hear God rather than waiting and relaxing. Striving is trying to hear a word. Performance is playacting. It is doing something that you know is not from the Lord. It's counterfeit. There is no anointing. That's how people know it is of the flesh. It is making up something. If we want God to use us, we need to have good character and to never do anything out of performance.

Sometimes, when we move in the gifts, we may feel pressure from people to give a word of knowledge. They start to expect that we will have a word. However, we should not feel burdened, for it is nothing that we can do to make it happen. When I was feeling this pressure one time, I heard God tell me that I should not feel like it's on *my* shoulders; it's on *His* and that the burden is indeed His. Just that word took such a weight off my shoulders. We just need to worship the Lord and love Him, and if He has a word for someone, He will know we are a willing vessel. We just need to yield so that He can work through us.

When we strive for a word, we look hard and search and try to hear God. But when we relax and just ask God if He has a word for someone, it usually will come right away. We don't have to say the right words or do anything. We don't have to search for a word from the Lord; we just yield and let God show us. The burden is not on us. As we yield, God takes it from there. We have no striving, no pressure, and no pride. That's when God does miracles. It's not as hard as we make it. Just as fear blocks us from hearing the Lord, striving does also. We should always remember to leave it in God's hands.

I was thinking about this one day when all of a sudden I heard in my spirit, "*Butterflies are free.*" When I asked God what this meant, He said that it's hard to catch a butterfly when you're chasing it. But when we're very still, it will come to us and land on us. Trying and working so hard to move in all God has for us never works because it is doing it in our own strength. As we surrender and yield to the Lord and just *be*, then we will have good success.

We need to show love, even when people are not being lovable. That's when miracles happen. As previously stated, we need to make sure that if we are dealing with an issue in our own lives that we are able to put it aside, yield to the Holy Spirit and put others' needs first. However, this becomes more difficult when the problem is in your own family. Our personal problem is then connected to the family problem, and everything gets all mixed up. When you have anger or hurt that you are personally dealing with and that hurt is for the person for whom you are praying—and now are attempting to pray for an entirely different matter that you both agree on—how mixed up is that!

For example, if you had a disagreement with your spouse over one thing and still haven't let go of that hurt or anger yet now you are praying with that spouse for another need that you both are in agreement with—let's say, healing—you are fighting within yourself. In order to be effective, you first need to let go of any anger, hurt, or bad feelings and let God work in you. You still need to put aside personal feelings and yield to the Holy Spirit.

On the one hand, you love the person and want him healed. On the other hand, you're still hurt and angry with that person. That's double-mindedness, and double-mindedness won't see victory. How do we handle it? If we can just stop and take a moment to get in God's presence, He will help us to truly let go of the bad feelings and put complete love back in our hearts. When we pray, we must forgive, as we learn in Mark 11:25. Unless we do this, we will not see victory.

God has a way of showing us what *we* did wrong if we will just yield to His voice. How many times when we ask God to show the person what they did wrong, He shows us we are the one to change or even apologize! It's the humility thing again, and it's God showing us that love is most important. What happens to the enemy when someone says they're sorry? The dart he stuck you with comes out of you and hits him. It wounds him. And it's a double whammy because it's coated with the forgiveness of the other person. That's a poison dart!

That's why it says in God's Word that we should not let the sun go down on our anger. Satan can't get ground then, and in fact, we disable him. The impact upon him is not just like a dart but more like a bomb. What the enemy meant for harm, God turns for good. Not only is he incapacitated and blessings can now flow, but we also learn and grow from it so that it is harder for him the next time he tries the same thing. What he tries to do again then will be like a red flag for us in the natural as to what he's trying to do in the spiritual.

When things get stressful and we wonder what is going on—a red flag—it's the enemy. Treat it as such with your sword. Anytime we turn and fight one another, it's spiritual and from the enemy. Be aware. Satan is a copycat. He saw how God turned the Israelites' enemies against one another, and he will try to do the same to us. He knows the power of unity. This should be no surprise to us, yet we go by our natural senses and get deceived easily. We look for natural causes, not spiritual, so it is as easy for Satan to confuse us as taking candy from a baby. We let our emotions control us. Anything that is not kind, loving, honest, praiseworthy, of good report, or having virtue is from the enemy.

Why is it so hard for us to see this? People live in a natural world, in a natural body, and were taught from childhood to pay more attention to our senses than our spirits. When our spirits rule our senses, then victory comes. To be a good vessel, we need both humility and love. It takes separating yourself from your emotions and your "pity party" and putting the other one's needs first. We can only do this when we look to God and His strength. He gives us the maturity and character we need to accomplish this. We cannot do this in our own strength, and God will give you plenty of times to get it right until your character equals your gifts. As the saying goes, "If at first you don't succeed…"

Last but certainly not least is our motivation for desiring the gifts. I put it last in this chapter because as the last thing you read, it will be the easiest to remember. Our motivation should not be because we want attention drawn to us or to feel important. If that is your motivation, you will not be pleasing to God—or to man, for that matter.

But if it's because you have God's heart of love for others and desire to bring God's words of love to them, you've got the right character. It's not about us! God doesn't need a particular person. He gives everyone gifts. All Christians can lay hands on the sick in Jesus's name. What it takes is compassion and love for others, a desire to have people feel God's presence in their lives to see His glory and His miracles.

It takes time in prayer, and it takes responsibility. It takes caring about others' needs and putting their needs first rather than wanting others to always meet your needs. It takes a giving spirit instead of just wanting to receive. Remember, we are God's messengers. We impart His presence in us to them. People need to know that we have credibility to speak God's word with honesty and integrity. God needs to know that He can trust us with His word. And we need to always be humble, never thinking that we did anything. We're just instruments God uses. What a privilege!

I was thinking about this one day after God gave me an encouraging word for someone. I felt God asking me then why I like to encourage others. I answered that it makes me happy. He then asked why I thought that was true. All of a sudden, I got the revelation that it was because Jesus is in me and that's what He likes to do! We learn about the Lord by the way we are because He is in us and we are in Him (John 17:21–23). We want to be like our Daddy and want others to know that He's their Daddy too. We want them to know that He's the best Daddy and cares about our every need.

6

———◆———✸———◆———

FIRE TAKES YOU HIGHER

GOING THROUGH THE
MOWING SO WE CAN GET TO GROWING

As I was in prayer one day, I got a vision of a hot air balloon. God showed me that for the balloon to rise in the sky, fire was needed. We often think of fire as in fiery trials. I'll write about that later in this chapter. But fire is also a character of the Holy Spirit. In Acts 2, we learn that when the day of Pentecost came, there was a rushing wind and there appeared tongues of fire upon the apostles. And they were filled with the Holy Spirit. In order for us to grow more in wisdom and understanding of God, we need to allow the Holy Spirit to fill us up with living water, which is also a characteristic of the Holy Spirit, and allow His fire to take us higher.

When natural water is thrown on a natural fire, it puts it out. When living water is added to the Holy Spirit's fire, it increases it. I believe that fire represents power and the water represents healing and fruitfulness. As the fire increases in us, so does healing and bearing fruit. As the living water flows, so the power will also increase. So, as the one will start to increase, so does the other. Like the old song about love and marriage, you can't have one without the other!

The Holy Spirit is wind, fire, and water; so if you have fire, you'll see fruit. The wind carries you and leads you in the right direction as the Holy Spirit guides you. His living water flows from us to bear fruit. It's a cycle that keeps increasing. Fire which takes you higher in wisdom and knowledge of the Lord, wind which leads you in the direction God wants you to go, and water which is His Spirit overflowing from you and bearing fruit.

Now, the lighter the balloon is, the higher it will rise. In order for us to go higher in the Lord, we sometimes need to throw out some baggage. The closer we get to the Lord, the more aware we will be of anything that needs to be gotten rid of. It's a good thing. God points out corrections to those He loves—His own. Without growth we can't move forward, and to continue to move forward, God corrects us so that we can develop into the person He wants us to be.

Growth is becoming more Christlike, more like our Lord. That is what intimacy is all about. God loves us with all our faults; but as we grow and shed the baggage, we get closer to Him, know Him more, and have more intimacy with Him. Therefore, we should not despise it when God reveals these things to us as it usually means new growth. It is just that before we go higher, sometimes some junk weighing us down has to be thrown out. Are we willing to go through the fire and take some pain of conviction?

When we blow up a balloon, it stretches. As we are filled with the Holy Spirit, God stretches us to reach new levels in Him. As we are filled more and more, God reveals more and more of Himself to us.

What about the fiery trials? Before growth, before breakthrough, there is usually a struggle. A baby chick has to break through his shell to get to his purpose. If someone breaks the shell for him, he will not build up the strength he needs to survive and dies. With no struggle, we stay in the same place. We do not build up the strength we need to fight the enemy.

Before we breakthrough to what God has for us, the enemy will usually put up obstacles, walls we need to break through. He wants to prevent us from getting all God has for us. There's a struggle and a battle, but unless we give up, there's always victory. God uses what the enemy meant for harm, for good.

I once saw a commercial in which a lady was wading through a cranberry bog. When I saw this, it came to me that we have to wade through a lot of stuff sometimes before the harvest comes! At one point, when it seemed we were being attacked really hard, I was crying out to God; I sensed Him telling me that when it seems all hell is breaking loose, all heaven is breaking loose too. Satan always puts up a fight before the blessings come. All the rain in heaven was breaking loose. God told me He always "reigns" on the enemy's parade! I had to chuckle at the pun. God does have a sense of humor. And then in His gentle way, He told me it was good to see me laugh again. God loves us and wants us to know He's with us in the trials.

God also allows us to be tested so that our faith will be strengthened and to help us grow. Every time we learn, it takes an effort. It's not always easy. If it were easy to learn, everyone would know everything. We learn through our trials and struggles, and then we can break out to a new level in the Lord. Can a baby chick grow if he's confined to a shell? Read what God's Word says in Romans 5:3–5:

> And not only so, but we glory in tribulations
> also: knowing that tribulation worketh patience;
> And patience, experience; and experience, hope:
> And hope maketh not ashamed; because the love
> of God is shed abroad in our hearts by the Holy
> Ghost which is given unto us.

God has to prepare our hearts to be ready for growth. It takes a bringing down sometimes before there can be a lifting up, to prevent pride from coming in. It's God's protection over us.

Satan does not stop trying to attack us, but as we grow in wisdom and knowledge, the attacks get shorter and weaker. We gain knowledge through experience, so even though the attacks may be hard, it's battle training, like boot camp. The people that can't make it through boot camp don't get in the army, so these trainings are necessary. God's army is different than armies in the natural because we know we win. Our boot camp then is simply standing strong and looking to Jesus in all circumstances and trusting Him when the trials come. After our boot camp, when the attacks come, we will have learned how to give the enemy the "boot." We learn to take the authority Jesus has given us. We can do this when we have revelation of who and Whose we are in order to take that authority. We know that Jesus lives in us, but we don't always realize this means His power is also in us. We walk in our flesh knowledge, what we can do. But we do not war against flesh but against principalities and powers, as we learn in Ephesians 6:12.

We have the Holy Spirit's power in us, but we have to know our authority and use it. The Lord has given it to us, but we have to choose whether or not to use it. It's like a lamp. We can turn it on to give light or just look at it and know it can give light. The power is there, but we have to use it, to do something with it to activate it. To use the lamp, we turn the switch. We need to use God's sword that He gave us—His Word. He is the Word, a Lamp unto our feet. We cover ourselves in the blood of Jesus and speak God's Word and praise Him. The enemy is no match for the Lord. We have to know, to grow.

Sometimes, we look at the trials going on in our lives, and we look at someone else who seems not to be going through any difficulties. The grass always looks greener on the other side of the fence. When I asked God about the trials we've had and why we went through some of them and others have not, He said, "You went through the mowing so you could get growing." The trials were the mowing, and they made our roots stronger and stronger so that we can stand strong as His promises to us are fulfilled.

Our roots need to be firmly planted in the Lord. This is necessary so that when the blessings come, we are prepared to receive them. How many have received a great blessing but were not prepared to handle it and it destroyed them because of lack of maturity? We hear this a lot with instant millionaires. God wants us to be prepared for all He has for us. I can now look back on things that have happened in our lives that I wondered why we went through them and now realize they prepared us for the blessings that were to come.

Preparedness results in permanence. The journey may be hard, but what matters is how we got there. What did we learn? How did we grow? The lessons learned along the way are priceless. They are of more value than riches. What I'm talking about here is wisdom. When something is gotten easily or handed to us or given to us, we do not have to learn anything to get it.

For example, we may be able to keep what is given to us as far as money, but we did not acquire the wisdom to know how to get more. We do not appreciate what it took to get it like those who worked for it appreciate it. Therefore, it does not result in a never-ending flow because it did not come from the wisdom we received. And once it's gone, it's gone. Like the well-known saying goes, "Easy come, easy go." So it's not always the end result that counts—it's what we learn along the way. It's all in the process. We should not be dismayed at the bumps on the road. We should not let them trip us up. God uses these bumps for His glory.

It's a continual process of dying and new growth. Just as the trees shed their leaves each fall to get ready for new growth, we die to our flesh so that new growth can occur. It's not just one death, for as we grow, we need to shed our leaves in different areas in our lives. As we look back over the years, we realize how much we've grown. We're not the same person as we were. Our thinking has changed, our priorities have changed, our goals have changed, our desires have changed, and even what we place importance on has changed.

It's a process that doesn't happen all at once. It happens through the testing and trials that remove the old leaves. One by one, old habits and ways of thinking are removed and replaced with new ways that come into alignment with the Word of God. It's true that major changes can and do occur at the time of salvation, but the changes don't stop there. That is only the beginning. It's the first shedding of leaves. As we go through seasons of shedding old ways and growth, we begin to not only grow but to produce fruit. It all starts with letting go.

Transitions—growth changes—can sometimes feel a little unsettling. I compare it to a plane hitting some turbulence before it gets to its destination. The plane hits turbulence because of changes in atmosphere. We can't *see* the turbulence, but we can *feel* it. When we are in the process of growing, the change may be causing some turbulence (unsettling feeling in our spirit), but it will smooth out soon. That's one reason God gives us a promise and a vision for our future. It helps us to see the end because getting there sometimes involves a little turbulence in our spirit. This is different than trials. Trials are what we go through in the natural. Turbulence is what we feel in our spirit. It's like the growing pains in teenagers where their bodies are changing as well as their emotions.

Our spirit goes through changes too. Just as this is normal for teenagers in the natural, it's normal in the spirit too. And in the spiritual, being a teenager does not have to do with chronological age. It has to do with growing and maturing spiritually. In fact, we can be as a teenager in the spirit in old age! In the spirit, there can also be more than one baby stage, teenage stage, and mature stage as we reach a new level of growth in different areas. It's the same with a vision. Between the baby stage when we first see it and the mature stage when we receive it, we may go through some teenage turbulence time. God is just getting us ready for the promise or for a new level of growth.

7

A FISH OUT OF WATER
CAN'T SURVIVE

We wonder why at times we feel like a fish out of water when nothing seems to be going the way we expected. God was showing me that on this earth, we are like fish out of water. Even in the womb we were surrounded by fluid, and then in birth, we were on our own, independent of our mothers.

When we are born again, we are again surrounded with water—this time, living water. It surrounds us and is in us. God's Word is in us, His Holy Spirit is in us, and therefore, we are in the spiritual river of living water. Though our flesh is in the world, our spirits are in the river, constantly being nourished and fed. Natural birth brings our bodies out of the water; rebirth brings our spirits back in. The flesh is a fish out of water; the spirit is the fish being bathed again in living water.

Because the flesh part of us is in the world, it struggles. But as our spirit is bathed in living water, it grows in peace. The more living water we have when on this earth, the more at peace we become. Living water satisfies the spirit just as natural water satisfies the flesh. Where there is no living water, the spirit can't grow and is suffocated like a fish out of water. The more world we have in us, the more flopping about and struggling to survive. The more living water in us, the more peace we have, for we have wisdom and direction from

God. The more we know, the more we grow. The more we grow, the more we know.

The Holy Spirit gives revelation, guidance, direction, conviction, and, most of all, love. We need revelation to expose deception, which leads to wrong thinking and behaviors. Guidance and direction are needed to get back on the right path. Conviction is needed to correct, and love is needed to come against the enemy's condemnation. Living water refreshes the weary soul and brings new life and growth. A well-watered soul exudes life, energy, and health. We are all a work in progress. When there's a crack in the clay, the potter will add more water and smooth it out. There are times when there are cracks in our spiritual wall, but all it takes is to add more living water to the vessel and it is smooth again.

Sometimes, after we have grown in one area, we go through a "dry" time. Everyone goes through the desert. It can be very unsettling, to say the least. We just should hang in there because, after being in the desert, the water will feel so much better. And know that when we are in the desert, we may not see evidence that God is there, we may not hear His voice, but He is still with us.

Sometimes, when God pulls back, it's only because He wants us to grow, to stretch us more. I remember when our daughter was very young and we wanted her to learn how to swim. We signed her up for group swimming lessons at the YMCA, but she would not move away from the side of the pool. We decided that she needed private lessons and found a swim instructor that she trusted. He started to move back so slowly that she did not realize she was going away from the side. He kept moving back as she started to move toward him. Finally, she realized she could swim to him. Like the swim instructor, I think God will move back so that we will move into a deeper level to be near Him. He says to trust Him and move forward into deeper water. He will always be there.

It is at those times, when we seek God more, that He is preparing us for a new level of growth. For everything, there is a season, and I believe this is true for growth seasons as well. Even in our everyday life there is a time for work and a time for sleep. Sleep is for rest to prepare us for the next day of work. This is also true in our spiritual life. Between each growth cycle, there is a resting cycle to prepare us for the next level of growth. It is during those times that we can mature in what we've just learned. It is like a crocus bulb. We plant it and it grows and flowers in spring. The bulb will then multiply so that the next season, there are more. God wants us to rest so that He can give us more of His wisdom, knowledge, and so that we can grow more in Him.

When growth happens, fish come to us for us to feed. An example of this is with the disciples. In the beginning, Jesus provided them with fish (Luke 5:4–7), then He multiplied the fish (Matt. 14:15–21), and then after Jesus was resurrected, He appeared to the disciples and they fed Him fish. He was hungry and they fed Him fish. (Luke 24:36–43)! Jesus provided them with fish in the beginning, and now they were feeding Him the fish.

When I thought about all these things, I realized that God provides us with what we need so that we can provide Him with what He needs—souls! He will send us fish (people) so that we can give Him fish (souls). I mentioned to God that He was talking to me a lot about fish. The answer I got was that He makes "fishers of men"; therefore, just as He made the disciples fishers of men, we are to do the same.

Fishing boats have anchors. When the anchor is down, the boat rests and does not move. When the anchor is up, the boat moves. But whether the anchor is up or down, it is always with the boat. Jesus is our anchor. Whether we're resting or moving forward (growing), He is always with us. The fish will come in either way.

8

GOD IS IN THE DRIVER'S SEAT DON'T BE A BACKSEAT DRIVER

When my husband and I were married only a few years, he gave me a little card that said Backseat Drivers' License. He was trying to tell me in a nice way that when he was in the driver's seat, I should not be telling him how to drive the car. Isn't that what we do to God sometimes? We want things done in our timing and in our way. But just as I could not control the car from the passenger's seat, we would do well to understand that we should not try to tell God how to do His job in working out His plan for our lives!

God brought to my attention a pinwheel we bought for our granddaughter. When He does this, I know that He wants to teach me or tell me something. When I asked, He told me that the wind blows the pinwheel to make it work. It starts to move and spins as the wind blows it. He then started comparing this vision to the Holy Spirit.

As the wind of the Holy Spirit blows over us, we start to move in the Spirit. The more wind, the more we feel the anointing upon us, the greater the move of the Holy Spirit. He told me to let the wind move me faster to new levels in Him. I told the Lord that I wasn't sure how to do this, and He responded that the pinwheel doesn't try to move nor does it try not to move; it yields to the wind. That what is needed is to continually yield to the Holy Spirit and that I have just begun to spin. Jesus holds the pinwheel, and when we catch the wind of the Holy Spirit, He takes us in the direction He wants us to go. He holds us and will not let go of us; therefore, we need not be afraid to move in all He has for us.

A few days after this teaching, God showed me a top spinning. He asked me if I knew how a top keeps its balance. I told Him that I thought it had to do with the wind's force as it moves. He told me that as it spins, it creates a force that keeps it balanced. Then He told me to let the Holy Spirit keep me in balance. As we move with the Holy Spirit, He will keep us in balance. He will not let us topple or fall. We will not go to the left or to the right, but we will stay centered on the Lord. We always need to keep our eyes on the Lord. He is the force that keeps us balanced. His Word keeps us upright.

And then I saw a hammock. When we are in a hammock, our eyes look up to the sky. We should look to the Lord in every situation. When we are in a hammock, we are resting and not doing anything. As we give control over everything in our lives to God, He will work out His plans for us. We need not to worry or fret but just to *rest* assured that He will take care of us. This goes for the burdens that we carry and the fear of God taking us out of our comfort level as He helps us to grow and move in the gifts of the Holy Spirit.

With these examples, God was teaching me about yielding to Him, with not only the direction and goals for our lives but especially when we move in the gifts of the Holy Spirit. It's so easy to bring our flesh into a word that God gives us. And it's not even that we do this for control but sometimes for fear of making a mistake of our flesh! Thus, the very thing we fear is what we do!

Let me explain what God taught me. When we get a word that we know from past experience is the way the Lord speaks to us, we should not reason it out. It's not about us; it's what God wants to do for someone. The word is not our flesh, but the reasoning part is. We should receive it as from the Lord, and we can ask Him for more specifics about it.

Asking Him is fine; reasoning it out in our own minds will bring us out of His presence. For then, the focus is on us and not the Lord or what He wants to do. That's the difference. We wait until we're in the Lord's presence, ask Him if He has a word for anyone, and don't think or use our reasoning when He responds. Once we reason, it's our flesh. Therefore, the very thing we were afraid of doing—moving in our flesh by reasoning—caused us to do it! The reasoning caused us to move in the flesh.

We may reason that we heard someone say they had that sickness a week ago. We may reason we felt like that a few days ago. If that were the case, there could be no healing words; for during the course of several weeks, there would be no words left to say! That's reasoning. We need to just open ourselves up to the Lord and receive the word without reasoning—because we asked Him.

Our fear of making a mistake could actually cloud our hearing. Reason interrupts us from hearing more about what God is saying because we are listening to ourselves instead. Reasoning cuts us off. We need to just step out in faith when God gives us a word, even if it doesn't make sense to us. God showed me an example that made this very clear. He said to let Him be in the driver's seat. When we start to reason, we are fighting with Him for the steering wheel. If we make a mistake, it's okay. However, keep in mind that reasoning takes us on our own path. Trusting God takes us where He wants us to go.

We try so hard to do everything right, but we don't have to try; we just need to be an open, willing vessel. Trying brings *us* into it. That's exactly the opposite of what it should be. We want to die to our self and let God flow *through* us. If we can remember that we are His vessel and to keep our vessels empty of flesh, then God can work through us easily and not have to push our stuff out of His way. We need to "keep it simple, sweetheart"!

This is also true when we want to accomplish a goal that the Lord has put on our hearts. The way we get off track is trying to do it without God's guidance. Doing is not bad unless it engulfs us and we focus on the *doing* and not on *being* in God's presence. It's true that doing is accomplishing something *for* God, but it has also got to be *with* God—not just for Him. So many of us get impatient and try to help God and do something that we feel will accomplish the goal faster. What we don't realize is that by doing it our way because we think that God is not moving fast enough, we take away God's glory. For God works it out in ways much better than we could have. (Isaiah 55:8–9).

The important thing is not to take our eyes off God and thereby making Him second in line to the task. As we yield to Him, we will see things we never thought possible. Total surrender is a sacrifice that is pleasing to the Lord. For it is in our yielding that He can accomplish His will for us.

FROM PINWHEEL TO WINDMILL

God wants us to go from pinwheel to windmill. We start our walks as pinwheels (children). The wind of the Holy Spirit moves the pinwheel. When we grow stronger in the Lord, we become like windmills, and we have more faith to believe God for miracles. We are filled with the Holy Spirit, His mighty anointing and power flowing through us. God wants us to be windmills, for all of us to go from pinwheel to windmill.

In the natural, the windmill itself has no power to move, and it needs the wind to move it. It's the same in the spiritual. The windmill is the instrument used. We need the wind of the Holy Spirit to flow through us. Natural windmills are generators of power (energy). Spiritual windmills are faith builders as people see God's power working through them. Faith is the fuel for miracles. Miracles beget miracles, for as people see a miracle, they have faith to believe for their miracle. One windmill can supply power (faith) to many. However, there are so many people yet so few windmills.

Remember this formula when comparing the natural to the supernatural:

NATURAL = WIND > WINDMILL > ENERGY > LIGHT
SUPERNATURAL = HOLY SPIRIT >
PERSON > FAITH > MIRACLES

Life is growth and growth is life. Spiritual growth comes after death—death to self. After death comes life. Death of our bodies is the beginning of life eternal. Death of self, giving our lives to the

birth. When we do this, we have new life, which means
..., which means the gifts we receive.

Gifts come with the price of growing in character, responsibility, and wisdom. We can't live without having growth of some kind,
and we can't grow in the Lord without death to self. Every living
thing grows, but growth in the Lord begins with death to self. We are
all growing in something. Is it that we are growing in the Lord...or
our own flesh?

> Peace comes on the top of a hill
> where now all is quiet and perfectly still.
> It's not in a bottle, neither pill filled nor wine
> but from a heart who's truly loved mine.
> To get to that hill takes not car, bus, or plane
> but merely the mention of Jesus's sweet name.
> He gave it all for you and for me;
> peace comes on a hill called Calvary.
> The yellow brick road will not get you home,
> but one that is blood stained is where you should
> roam.
> So, choose very wisely the path you should go;
> the one that looks good isn't necessarily so.
> It isn't by touch or by sight or by sound
> that tells if you're standing on solid ground
> but that still, small voice that says, "Come over here,
> "I'll show you the path that is perfectly clear."
> So, take heed and listen and then you will know
> the perfect direction in which you should go.

May you always keep God in the driver's seat!

If you have never given your life to the Lord and want the intimate relationship that you have been reading about, then pray this prayer and mean it in your heart:

> Lord Jesus, I believe that You are the Son of God and that You died on the cross for my sins. Come into my life, be my Lord and Savior, and I will follow You all the days of my life. Thank You for forgiving my sins and thank You that I now have eternal life. Amen.

You may not feel any change in yourself right away, but just receive the gift of salvation by faith. Confess with your mouth that you have received Jesus's precious gift of eternal life. For it is by faith and receiving God's free gift of grace that you are saved. Get a Bible and read it every day. Go to a Holy Spirit–filled, Bible-teaching church and join the fellowship of the family of Christ.

Now let me pray a prayer over you.

> The Lord bless thee and keep thee. The Lord make his face shine upon thee, and be gracious unto thee. The Lord lift up his countenance upon thee, and give thee peace. (Numbers 6:24–26)

> *"If we live in the Spirit, let us also walk in the Spirit."*

> —Galatians 5:25

OTHER RESOURCES

Books

Lessons I learned from the Lord.

Magazine Articles

Inner Voice Magazine—www.innervoicemag.com

Titles

"Listen to His Heartbeat"
"Just Whistle"
"End of Your Rope"
"God's Love Notes"
"Do-Overs"
"Fragrance of Fall"
"The Sparkle and Sound of Crystal"

Blogs

Read Evelyn Lang's encouraging and insightful blogs at
www.evelynlangbooks.com

About the Author

Evelyn Lang is an anointed Christian author and speaker who has helped people have victory in their lives. She is the author of *Lessons I learned from the Lord* and has written several articles for *Inner Voice Magazine*. Evelyn has been a guest on *Christian Television Network's It's Time for Herman and Sharron, The Harvest Show*, and local cable television.

Her book, *Lessons I learned from the Lord* was featured on *The Elijah List* and in *SpiritLed Woman Magazine's PowerUp!*

Evelyn acknowledges that God often uses "little ol' me's" to accomplish His purposes.

Thank you for purchasing this book.
I pray that it has been a blessing to you.

A portion of the sale of this book is donated to charity.

CPSIA information can be obtained
at www.ICGtesting.com
Printed in the USA
LVOW03s1521220218
567559LV00003B/630/P